FOR WANT OF A FIR TREE

UKRAINE UNDONE

FOR WANT OF A FIR TREE
UKRAINE UNDONE

by
Frédérick Lavoie

Translated by Donald Winkler

For Want of a Fir Tree: Ukraine Undone was originally published in French in 2015 as *Ukraine à fragmentation*, by La Peuplade of Chicoutimi, Québec.
Copyright © 2015, Frédérick Lavoie
Translation © 2018, Donald Winkler

All rights reserved. No part of this book may be reproduced, for any reason or by any means, without permission in writing from the publisher.

Cover image: Chris G. Collison
Cover design: Debbie Geltner
Book design: Tika eBooks

Library and Archives Canada Cataloguing in Publication

Lavoie, Frédérick, 1983-
[Ukraine à fragmentation. English]

       For want of a fir tree : Ukraine undone / Frédérick Lavoie ; translated by Donald Winkler.

Translation of: Ukraine à fragmentation.
Issued in print and electronic formats.
ISBN 978-1-988130-93-4 (softcover).--ISBN 978-1-988130-94-1 (HTML).--
ISBN 978-1-988130-95-8 (HTML).--ISBN 978-1-988130-96-5 (PDF)

       1. Ukraine Conflict, 2014-. 2. Ukraine--History--21st century.
I. Winkler, Donald, translator II. Title. III. Title: Ukraine à fragmentation. English.

DK508.852.L3813 2018   947.7086 C2018-901280-3
                                            C2018-901281-1

Printed and bound in Canada.

The publisher gratefully acknowledges the support of the Government of Canada through the Canada Council for the Arts, the Canada Book Fund, and Livres Canada Books, and of the Government of Quebec through the Société de développement des entreprises culturelles (SODEC).

We acknowledge the financial support of the Government of Canada through the National Translation Program for Book Publishing, an initiative of the *Roadmap for Canada's Official Languages 2013-2018: Education, Immigration, Communities*, for our translation activities.

Linda Leith Publishing
Montreal
www.lindaleith.com

To Artyom
and to all those
who did nothing to deserve this

PROLOGUE

ARTYOM

ANDREA:

Unhappy is the land with no heroes.

[…]

GALILEO:

No. Unhappy is the land that needs heroes.

Bertolt Brecht

Now I know. When Grad rockets rain down around you, you have a better chance of escaping unharmed if you find yourself in the direct line of a projectile's impact than if you're behind it or off to the side. When it strikes the ground at an oblique angle, the rocket propels its shrapnel at that same angle. It's logical, but I'd never thought about it. I'd never had to think about it. I found myself pondering the question for the first time when a salvo of Grads split Mariupol's sky open one Saturday afternoon at the end of January. I was standing in front of the still fresh ruins of a computer store in the Kyivsky Market. Its owner was assessing the damage. On the outer road, the ground was still soaked with the blood of an anonymous shopper, killed in one of the morning's explosions. I quickly ducked into a shop to take shelter. The place was empty, with no furniture or merchandise. As before, the firing was coming most probably from the east. Was it better for me to hug the wall on that side? Or on the contrary, to stay near the door facing west? Undecided, I curled myself into a ball in the middle of the room.

What I also didn't know was that once the attack's noise reached my ears, I was already safe. Grad rockets travel twice as fast as sound. The gunners had already made an adjustment, and had hit their target, a military roadblock four hundred metres to the north, rather than the residential neighbourhood where they'd caused thirty deaths four hours earlier.

Artillery firing is not an exact science. Knowing its laws helps you to grasp the dangers it presents, but not to protect yourself. I'd just been lucky.

Unlike you.

★★★

I captured the absurdity of your funeral in a photograph. There you are, your brow circled by a headband and its prayer, lying in your little blue coffin mounted on two stools. Your plush rabbit is sleeping by your side. Your legs are covered in red carnations. The cemetery is wrapped in fog. The ground is covered in snow. Father Mikhail has just interrupted his funeral oration yet again. This time, it's not nearby mortar fire that drowns out his voice. It's the infernal din caused by two trucks armed with multiple Grad rocket launchers, passing by just a metre behind his back. Almost everyone has turned to look at them. Only your grandmother cannot bring herself to take her eyes off you.

It will have hounded you right into your tomb, this vile war, Tyomochka. No, but how ironic. You in your coffin. Your grandmother's tears. The priest's oration. And the Grads moving about for no obvious reason within the cemetery. The very weapon to which you owe your death is attending your funeral, uninvited. A funeral that would not have happened if on Sunday morning - while you were having breakfast in the sitting room, waiting for your father to return from his night shift at the foundry - a gunner on the other side of the front line had not pressed a button in hopes of destroying his enemy's artillery, the same that was claiming to defend you and that had had the bright idea of positioning itself near your house, from where it fired towards the enemy emplacements, and in so doing struck houses just as innocent as your own.

You're collateral damage, Artyom. Nothing more, nothing less. No one wanted your death, but you died anyway. You must be asking yourself why. You were just the right age for "whys." So I'm going to explain it to you. I'm going to explain why on January 18, 2015, at 8:10 in the morning, on 5 Ilinskaya Street in Donetsk, your life was cut short after four years, four months, and fourteen days, by an error in the trajectory of a Grad rocket, without it altering in the least the course of the war. But I'm warning you right away: none of my explanations will be able to silence the tireless outflow of your "whys". Nothing that I recount will carry enough meaning to satisfy your simple childhood logic. There is no "because," no historical, political, or military argument, no virtuous feeling of moral superiority on the part of this war's protagonists, the protagonists of any war, that can justify, even in part, the usurpation of your right to life. You were innocent and you remain so. They were all guilty and they still are. All those who have reached the age of reason and who continue despite everything to celebrate death, to promote hate, to promulgate what is false, to load weapons and hope for anything but the unconditional termination of combat.

It's to you, Tyoma, that I want to relate what I've seen, learned, and felt in Ukraine, parading my naive, childlike "whys" before the annihilation of man by man. You won't understand everything, of course. The absurd is a concept that one can only begin to grasp at the age of eight or nine. But at least you won't try to justify the unjustifiable in the name of an ideal or a flag, to view all the complexities as a simple Machiavellian plan on the part of the enemy. You will perhaps understand that a sequence of events can be logical without being planned by anyone in particular; that your country was able to drift from peace into war in the space of a few months through an absurd set of circumstances that on one side and the other, blinded by a thousand and one petty considerations, no one was able to defuse. You will see that war is a trap into which human nature can easily allow itself to fall.

It goes without saying that you didn't deserve to die. You at least deserve to know what led to your death.

FRÉDÉRICK LAVOIE

PART 1

CHAOS THEORY

For want of a nail the shoe was lost.
For want of a shoe the horse was lost.
For want of a horse the rider was lost.
For want of a rider the message was lost.
For want of a message the battle was lost.
For want of a battle the war was lost.
For want of a war the kingdom was lost.

And all for the want of a horseshoe nail.

ANCIENT PROVERB

Chapter 1

THE FIR TREE

You may not believe me, but it all began with an argument over the erection of a New Year's fir tree seven hundred kilometres from where you live. It was the end of November, more than a year before your death. A few thousand people were gathered on *Maidan Nezalezhnosti*, Kyiv's Independence Square. There they had set up tents. They were angry with their president. Viktor Yanukovych had just pulled back from ratifying an association agreement with the European Union. Just like that, two days before the ceremony, after having vaunted for months the merits of the accord. He now claimed that its coming into force would be a disaster for the Ukrainian economy. According to him, the reforms demanded by the EU and the International Monetary Fund in exchange for loans and the opening up of markets would do too much damage to be worth the trouble. Too much damage for his corrupt friends above all, but also, it's true, for ordinary Ukrainians in the short and medium term. The disruption could cost him politically as well. Yanukovych had to think about his re-election because, despite its failings, Ukraine was still a democratic nation. The status quo was less of a risk.

To this picture you had to add Russia, Ukraine's most important economic partner. The prospect of seeing its neighbour ally itself with the European giant disturbed it greatly. And so Moscow had threatened Kyiv with cutbacks in its imports and the levying of new taxes in the event of an agreement being signed with its rivals. Then at the last minute, Russia made a tempting counter-offer: a loan as generous as that of the Europeans, but without the constraints. There would be no need to put in place any reforms. Ukraine would be saved from bankruptcy for a few more months, and the president could sail on without fear towards the next election. Yanukovych accepted and turned his back on Europe, returning to his former loves.

If I am explaining all this to you, Artyom, it's so that you'll understand that prior to the great patriotic speeches, the weapons and the deaths, there were columns of figures and electoral strategies.

Politics is a stage that is no stranger to theatrical effects. There's nothing new in the fact that a government elected by the people can go back on its promises for good or bad reasons. But some turnabouts are more clumsy than others. At one minute to midnight, in a socio-political context that is already very tense, when grievances have accumulated sufficiently, this kind of backtracking can turn out to be the last straw.

★★★

So that you may better understand what follows, and the story of the fir tree that will ensue, let me go back even further into the past.

Today's Ukraine is a historical construction. Its borders bear the scars of annexations, conquests, and administrative reorganizations put into effect by the empires - Austro-Hungarian, Ottoman, Polish, Russian, and Soviet - that shunted it back and forth up to its independence in 1991. As a result, the country is made up of inhabitants with a variety of cultural, genetic, linguistic, and historical pasts. Your ancestors, for example, doubtless arrived in the Donbas coal fields from Russia in the massive industrialization of the region during the second half of the nineteenth century. Installed in the city, they probably did not suffer too much during the *Holodomor*, the great famine of the 1930s, created artificially by the Soviets. It was primarily the peasants, most of Ukrainian ethnicity, who were decimated by the millions when the authorities began to confiscate their harvests. Stalin considered them too nationalist and too resistant to the collectivization of farmland that he had undertaken. To weaken them and to bring them to heel, he decided to starve them.

During the Second World War, your great grandfather, a coal miner, was no doubt called up to fight under the Red Army flag. He even, most probably, combatted the Ukrainian nationalist insurgents who wanted to drive off the Soviets and recreate a Ukrainian state. The only independent Ukraine that had existed up to that point had lasted barely three years, at the end of the First World War, before being broken up and once again absorbed by the neighbouring empires. To revive it, the insurgents had briefly allied themselves with the Nazis, the enemies of their enemies. Your great grandfather had perhaps been one of the Soviet soldiers who ultimately marched on Polish Galicia, populated primarily by Ukrainians, to annex it and make of it what is today the western part of Ukraine.

On February 27, 1954, less than a year after Stalin's death, he'd certainly read on page one of *Pravda* that the new secretary-general of the USSR Communist Party, Nikita Khrushchev, had decided to present the Soviet Socialist Republic of Ukraine with a gift: the Crimean peninsula, which had up to that point been Russian. This administrative decision did not change much at the time, since Ukraine and Russia were part of the same country. It's once the union broke down that the problems began.

So it was that in 1991, Ukraine became independent. This country, which had only briefly existed beforehand, and then in a very different form, had to forge a national identity for itself in order to justify its post-Soviet existence. Within its borders there lived Ukrainians, Russians, Tatars, Greeks, and many other ethnic groups. But most of its citizens were ethnically and linguistically Ukrainian; that is what set it apart. This language was also the primary common denominator for all those ethnic Ukrainians divided half a century earlier between

Poland and the Soviet Union. And so Ukrainian would become the official language. However, in the east, in the south, and in Crimea, the vast majority of the population was Russian-speaking. Even in the capital, Kyiv, Russian was often the favoured language for day-to-day communication. But Ukraine was Ukraine and not Russia. To give status to Russian, the language of the "colonizer," of the "former occupier," would risk compromising the identity of the country. You could not ban the mother tongue of a third of the inhabitants, but neither would it be officially recognized.

Despite this, your family, like most Russian speakers, chose to remain in Ukraine. New borders appeared without the population being consulted. Your house had not changed its location for all that. People continued to live more or less as before. No one stopped them from speaking Russian at home, at work, in the street, or even at school. They just had to manage to fill out certain forms in Ukrainian. All was well: retirees still received their pensions, hospitals still cared for the sick, the mines functioned, the foundries too. It was possible to put bread on the table, and to live more or less as before.

For a handful of wily Russian speakers in the east, the transition from Communism to a market economy even made it possible for them to enrich themselves. They laid hands on the choice Soviet mining and industrial operations that the new Ukrainian state wanted to unload. They did so often under dubious circumstances, sometimes frankly criminal. But in the end this control over heavy industry gave these new oligarchs considerable political heft on the national scene, which extended to the Russian-speaking minority in general.

Let's now return to the month of November, 2013. Viktor Yanukovych has been in power for almost four years. He is the unofficial representative of the clan of Russian-speaking oligarchs from Donbas, in the country's industrial heartland. He is also perceived as Moscow's puppet. That is why his sudden willingness to ally himself with the European Union has surprised many: if even the most pro-Russian chief of state that Ukraine had known since its independence has become pro-European, that means that the whole country is marching in lockstep towards a Western future.

But lo, at the last minute, Yanukovych changes his mind. For the demonstrators gathered on the Maidan a few hours after that announcement, Ukraine has fallen to its knees once more before Russia. The president has destroyed their dream of one day becoming part of "civilized Europe." Among those involved in Euromaidan - that's the name they gave to their movement - there are businessmen who have had enough of large-scale and petty corruption, and of the Soviet bureaucracy in which the country is still mired two decades after independence. There are students who want a degree that has some value outside of Ukraine, and a passport that allows them to travel abroad with ease. There are also radical soccer fans, Russian-speaking for the most part, but Ukraine patriots to the point of being chauvinistic. And there are hardcore nationalists, some of whose grandfathers had joined the resistance against the Soviet army during the Second World War. There is, in short, a cocktail of Ukrainian citizens who are disillusioned and angry. People who thought that the country was heading towards a better future - European and not Russian, democratic and not authoritarian, independent and not compliant - and who feel that the president has just sold off that future for a few dozen billion Russian rubles.

★★★

Now to the fir tree.

Every year, as the holiday season approaches, Kyiv's city hall installs a giant New Year's fir tree on the Maidan. In fact, it's really a metal structure, a tree in name only, vaguely resembling a conifer. It's the last day of November. The demonstrations on Independence Square have lasted for more than a week. The authorities want to put up their artificial tree, but the protesters are standing in their way. At dawn, when only a few hundred campers are left, the anti-riot forces surround the Maidan. Despite their ultimatum, the protesters refuse to leave. Then there's an incident. A policeman attacks a protester with his club. Or perhaps a protester first lobs a blunt object in the direction of a policeman? Either way, the result is the same: everything deteriorates. A few hours later, dozens are wounded. The country is in a state of shock. Since independence, demonstrations have always ended peacefully.

There have been a few altercations and arrests, but never violence on that scale. During the Orange Revolution in 2004 - the greatest grassroots movement the country had seen up to then - the demonstrators and the powers that be ultimately reached a compromise: the fraudulent election was annulled, and there was a new vote, won by the candidate supported by the people in the street. After a standoff that lasted for weeks, everyone had gone home, heads held high or bowed low, without a scratch. This time, the violence has made it much more difficult to find a way out of the crisis. All because it was of the utmost urgency, supposedly, to raise up an artificial fir tree on the country's central square so that children like you could go and marvel at it and get to meet *Ded Moroz*[1]. I know, now that we've seen what followed, and what happened to you, the gravity of that "national drama" seems overblown. But the escalation had to start somewhere.

★★★

According to the principles of chaos theory, a tiny shift in initial conditions in a non-linear system can generate unforeseeable and tragic results in the long term. Even if every wingbeat of a butterfly does not spawn a tornado, it's still possible, in theory, that a single one of them may result in a displacement of air that will create just such an atmospheric disturbance.

---

[1] "Father Frost" is the Soviet equivalent of the Western Santa Claus.

In the non-linear system that was Ukraine, the violent incident surrounding a fir tree was just the minute alteration the socio-political situation needed to trigger hostilities.

A butterfly had flapped its wings. A little wisdom might still have staved off the catastrophe, might have righted things. The tornado might have been nipped in the bud.

As you know, that was not to be.

For want of a fir tree, the peace was lost.

Chapter 2

THE REVOLUTION

It's not unusual, pretty much everywhere in the world, for demonstrations to lead to confrontation and produce wounded or dead. Sometimes, the scenes of violence go on for days before, finally, the protest leaders sit down with the government and find common ground. On other occasions, the movement dies out on its own, either because the fervour among the populace has diminished, or because the protesters fear even harsher repression on the part of the authorities were they to defy them further. More rarely, the street succeeds in overturning the government and seizing power.

The episode surrounding the New Year's fir tree might have remained an isolated incident. Why did it not? Why did it lead rather to a revolution, and to war?

If you were to ask *them*, they would all give you the same answer: "It's the other side that started it. They'd been plotting their move for a long time. They executed a plan whose goals were very precise. All we did was defend ourselves."

At the risk of disappointing you, Tyoma, the reality is

much more banal than their Manichean fantasies. If your country went into this spiral, it's because human beings reacted like human beings to events that were beyond them; it's because, blinded by both their fears and their ideals, they did not know how to foresee the consequences of their actions. Their euphoria was of short duration, and the result, worse than the worst of their nightmares.

★★★

A few hours after the clash on the last day of November, the fir tree's metal structure has already risen over the Maidan. The tents have been torn down, the protesters are in detention or at home. That might have been the end of it, with repression winning the day. A few intrepid individuals might have dared to venture out one more time to defy the angry truncheons of a regime that was more intransigent than ever, but the faint-hearted majority would have stayed safely at home. Except that instead of stoking the terror, Yanukovych defused it with this astonishing reaction: he apologized to the wounded demonstrators, condemned the brutality of the police, and promised that such excesses would not repeat themselves. His act of contrition does not ease the tensions. It gives fury a second wind.

"The regime has admitted its guilt! Let's be done with it!"

I'd really like to be able to tell you, Artyom, that in this world here below, *mea culpas* curb hatred rather than incite it. But when minds are inflamed, a sin confessed comes nowhere near to being pardoned. Most of the time it's thrown back in the face of the one who has admitted to it, for not having wanted or been able to avert it.

The next day, the protesters assembled in Kyiv's city centre are more numerous than ever. The repression has enraged them. Yanukovych's excuses have made them believe that he would not a second time resort to force. Power has beat a retreat, and they advance. Again they occupy the Maidan, and even the Kyiv city hall. The police have orders to intervene as little as possible. After hours of champing at the bit, they finally make their move when the demonstrators try to march on the presidential headquarters. By the end of the day, Euromaidan has retaken the territory it lost, and has even occupied hundreds more square metres downtown.

Over the following weeks, between intervals of calm, the same sort of confrontation repeats itself. The growing escalation of anger and blame makes each new cycle more violent than the previous one: the street is up in arms. The powers that be bide their time, hoping things will die down, then grow impatient and find a pretext for a crackdown: a fir tree, the adoption of a law prohibiting assemblies, an affront on the part of the demonstrators, an "anti-terrorist" measure. The street is scandalized. The powers apologize and awkwardly reach out to the movement. Opposition politicians will negotiate in the name of the street. An agreement is reached, but the politicians do not represent the street. The street refuses to be led. It doesn't want another Orange Revolution with politicians involved, like that of nine years earlier. It knows now that once in power, politicians invariably betray the revolution's ideals and adopt the corrupt practices of the old regime. The street swears that that won't happen again. That's why it refuses to have leaders at its head. Except that headless, the street is only a heart. It's deaf to appeals to reason, ignores strategic considerations. Even when those in power agree to most of its demands, it refuses to bend. It's not willing to make any concessions. The struggle becomes an end in itself. The street expresses itself in songs and slogans.

"Glory to Ukraine! Glory to the heroes! Freedom or death!"

In no time at all, the most extreme voices drown out the more moderate. Patriotism is measured in decibels and degrees of bravura. When small groups decide to act out, no one can stand in their way. They're the minority amid a pacifist sea, but they lead the charge. They push the street to defy power more and more, and power responds with increased repression. In January, the level of violence moves up a notch. The police start bringing out their firearms and using them. The demonstrators add Molotov cocktails to their arsenal of sticks and bricks. With each new confrontation, what those in power lose in legitimacy, the street gains in radicalism. It's David who refuses to compromise, but it's Goliath who crushes those weaker than himself. The wounded become the dead. The dead become heroes. The elected president, a "dictator." The demonstrators, "terrorists." Since the episode of the fir tree, the street and power communicate only through violence. It's a total impasse. The confrontation reaches its climax in mid-February. In this battle, the policemen are not the only ones with guns. Some demonstrators have laid hands on them. The fighting lasts for four days. Then, on the morning of the fifth, nothing. Kyiv awakes to silence. The streets at the city centre are strewn with dozens of bodies. The weapons are mute. The anti-riot units have left the capital. The president has fled. The street has won.

★★★

The fall of a regime is often attributable less to a protest movement's manifest victory, than to the crumbling of a power structure.

A few hours before fleeing, Yanukovych brought together the leaders of the political opposition for new talks. European ministers attended the meeting in their capacity as mediators. The situation was grave. The country's stability was threatened more than ever. The president had to a large degree been responsible for his own debacle, and was now trying to put things back in order. This pattern was typical of him. Viktor had known a difficult youth. He'd grown up in a world where you won respect with your fists. He'd spent two and a half years behind bars for theft, assault and battery. His immediate reaction when there was a crisis was to crush his adversary. Now he was no longer a provincial hoodlum. He was the head of a democratic state with European aspirations. But he always seemed to understand too little, too late, that in this world respect is won differently.

Still believing that he could demonstrate his good faith, he accepted several of the demands made by those facing him across the negotiation table. He agreed to modify the constitution in such a way as to reduce his own powers, to form a government of national unity, and to hold early elections. But the concession that led to his downfall was altogether different: he gave the green light to an investigation whose goal was to arrest and judge those policemen responsible for the massacre of recent days. To survive politically, he was prepared to sacrifice his most loyal allies, those who had been defending him for three months at the risk of their lives. Naively, he imagined that this ultimate compromise would calm the demonstrators, and restore his respectability. Even more naively, he seems to have believed that his staunch protectors would continue to defend him even as he was preparing to hand them over to a crowd thirsting for revenge.

Learning of Yanukovych's treachery, the police realized that they now had to think about saving their own skin, rather than his. If the president remained in power, they would be judged and condemned. Yet if the street carried the day, they would be treated even more harshly. And so they all fled the capital swiftly to seek refuge in regions largely hostile to Euromaidan, such as Crimea and Donbas.

Once the forces of order had deserted the presidential headquarters and ceased guarding the chief of state's residence in the Kyiv suburbs, Yanukovych knew that he was no longer safe anywhere. The only option he had left was to flee in turn towards the eastern part of the country, and ultimately, to Russia.

★★★

During those three revolutionary months, your father continued to go to work every day at the foundry. The country's future was being weighed in the balance far from there, in Kyiv, in a perimeter of a few square kilometres enclosing the Maidan, the parliament, the council of ministers, and the presidential headquarters. Where you lived, in Donetsk, there were during this period a few pro- and anti-Euromaidan demonstrations. But, far from the centres of power, they had little influence on the course of events. Periodically, Yanukovych's Party of Regions brought its supporters out to the statue of Lenin, on the square of the same name. Many of them were paid to take part in those gatherings, and civil servants were bluntly ordered to turn up. Still, your parents' concerns, and those of millions of others, as to what was happening on the Maidan in Kyiv, were very real. The situation was just not yet perilous enough for them to parade their fears out in the open. All the more so in that if they supported Yanukovych, it was less out of love than by default. He and his gang were corrupt, everyone knew it, but they remained the defenders of the Russian speakers' interests on the national political scene: of Donbas's miners, metal workers, retirees, and oligarchs.

The more the violence escalated during the clashes in the capital, the more concerned the residents of your city became. The Russian television networks, their main source of information, featured *ad nauseam* the few ultra-nationalists with neo-Nazi affinities on the front lines of the Maidan battles. They were much in the minority, but they were also very radical, and determined to attain their goals. What would happen if they ever took power?

When Euromaidan finally overthrew the president, this question was no longer hypothetical. The worst could happen. While millions of Ukrainians celebrated the revolution's victory, millions of others where you were in Donbas, but also in the south of the country and in Crimea, were sceptical. They wanted to be reassured. They couldn't understand: what right had the demonstrators had to oust a president who, while certainly corrupt, had been democratically elected? For them this amounted to a coup d'état.

Arguments on one side or the other went on for hours. The revolutionaries said that Viktor Yanukovych saw his moral right to govern start to slip away the day when the first baton came down on the head of a demonstrator in November, and that he lost it for good when the first protester was killed by a bullet in January. For them, the president's hands had thereafter been stained with the blood of his people, and the people had a patriotic duty to bring him down in order to save the Ukrainian state from dictatorship. Yanukovych's supporters, for their part, countered that the president was fulfilling his moral and legal obligations by preventing the putschists, by all possible means, from usurping power unconstitutionally. It was Yanukovych who was trying to save the Ukrainian state, not the revolutionaries. He had even offered compromises to the malcontents on a number of occasions, and they had all been refused.

In short, each found a way to be in the right. They would brandish, each in turn, a range of laws to plead their case, and would fill the legal holes in their arguments by appealing to virtue and common sense. But *a posteriori*, they would all be wrong. Because, while they were busy blaming the Other and labouring to prove their own legitimacy, they did nothing to forestall the catastrophe looming on the horizon.

The revolution had resulted in Ukraine losing its balance. The country was divided more than ever. Irreparable moves had been made. Citizens had died. Violence had been used as a political weapon. What the country needed was a national dialogue, hands held out, a calming. The days to come would be crucial. But what everyone, at that precise moment, wanted above all, was to be right.

Sadly, Tyoma, in great moments, people often show themselves to be very small.

For want of peace, the balance was lost.

Chapter 3

FILLING THE VOID

I don't think I'm exaggerating when I say that the future of post-revolutionary Ukraine - and by extension, yours - played itself out over one February weekend. On Friday night, the president left the capital. Monday morning, the void left by his departure was filled. In between, those newly in power were busy confirming the fears of those who distrusted them.

On Saturday, February 22, 2014, the protesters breach the iron doors of the presidential headquarters without meeting any resistance. Meanwhile, two streets away, the members of parliament are meeting in an extraordinary session. The few MPs present from the Party of Regions, up to now loyal to the head of state, rally to the revolutionaries.

"Glory to Ukraine! Glory to the heroes!"

The parliament dismisses Yanukovych on the pretext that in fleeing the capital, he has voluntarily abandoned his post. (The president, for his part, claims that his impromptu trip to Kharkiv is linked to his duties.) The opposition MPs take power. They promise to honour the ideals of Euromaidan, now rebaptized the "Revolution of Dignity." A government and an interim head of state are chosen. Technically, there has been no coup d'état, but a simple reorganization of the power structure among the elected.

The parliamentarians throw themselves into a marathon legislative session. One law at a time, they try to forestall any possibility of a step backwards.

They erase the past. The Soviet red star, which still adorns the building where they are sitting, is taken down that very day.

They avenge the dead. The *Berkut*, the anti-riot forces that opposed the protesters before fleeing the capital a few hours earlier, is dismantled.

They get their own back. They vote for the immediate liberation of the former prime minister, Yulia Tymoshenko, the sworn enemy of Yanukovych, detained for the last two years for misappropriation of funds and the abuse of power.

The next day, Sunday, February 23, as the marathon continues, a nationalist deputy rises. He has awaited this moment for a long time. He proposes the revocation of the law on languages, adopted eighteen months earlier, amid controversy. Under this law, Russian was granted the status of a regional language where it was spoken by more than 10 per cent of the population. For the first time since independence, Russian speakers like those in your family saw their mother tongue officially recognized. Now, twenty-four brief hours after the shift in power, they must prepare to lose this meagre recognition.

<u>FOR</u> 232

<u>AGAINST</u> 37

<u>ABSTAINING</u> 2

<u>DID NOT VOTE</u> 43

"Motion adopted!"

In voting, the deputies in favour feel that they are simply reinstituting the law that had been in effect during the first twenty-one years of the country's existence. Some of them perhaps appreciate the great symbolic significance of the gesture they have made, but they have obviously not measured the potential consequences. The euphoria of victory is a drug that alters one's apprehension of danger.

Imagine your parents' reaction.

That night, they probably watch television. All of the hyperactive parliament's decisions adopted during the day are announced. Among them, they note in particular that the deputies have revoked the law on languages, which gave them access to public services in Russian. How predictable. This measure affects them directly, more than all the others. You speak Russian at home, as does your father at the foundry. Your parents' friends and neighbours are Russian-speaking. They went to school in Russian. In Donetsk, they do their errands in Russian. Their mother tongue is what distinguishes them from the Ukrainian majority with which they have little contact, since in your city, that majority is a minority. Now your parents remember those news reports featuring the Maidan neo-

Nazis, some of whom have drawn inspiration from previous generations who joined forces with the fascists to fight your own forebears during the Second World War. Now the descendants of those nationalists have assumed power after violent clashes. And barely are they in place – while there are so many crucial decisions that must be made to deal with the urgent problems facing the country, when there are so many measures to be taken to ensure a better future for all Ukrainian citizens – than they hasten to wipe from the slate one of the only political achievements of which the Russian-speaking minority can boast. Your parents, your neighbours, whole regions envision the worst scenarios. Will these ultranationalists make them pay for the crimes of the deposed president, who defended their interests? Will they prevent the descendants of the soldiers of the Soviet "army of occupation" from honouring the sacrifices of their grandparents? This repeal of the law on languages is the first step towards the country's descent into fascism, they tell themselves. The symbol is too telling for it to be a coincidence. We must act before it's too late.

***

When a nation sails through troubled waters at a decisive moment in its history, it sometimes happens that a leader emerges who can guide it to safe harbour. His fineness of spirit, his gift for empathy, his unifying vision, his sense of justice, and his moral force, serve to right a craft that a divided people, prey to its most primitive instincts, was about to see founder. Mohandas K. Gandhi, Martin Luther King Jr., Nelson Mandela, Václav Havel. They are among the few to have emerged at the right moment, and to have warded off a catastrophe. More often nations are left to their own devices, or worse, fall into the hands of leaders as petty and vengeful as a roused crowd hounding a condemned man to the gallows.

The Revolution of Dignity did not produce a leader worthy of its name or of its noblest ambitions. The conquerors exhibited the commonplace arrogance of victors. As soon as they could, pressing a few buttons in parliament, they hastened to slake their thirst for vengeance. Except that the "losers" they wanted to punish lived within the borders of their own country. They were Ukrainian citizens like all others. Even if their goal was not to punish them - the revolutionaries will swear that it was not - that is how their actions were perceived by those who suffered the consequences.

In troubled times, perceptions outweigh intentions. Very soon, the sweet spoils of revenge were to cost the country its unity.

For want of balance, unity was lost.

Chapter 4

THE PENINSULA

The Crimean peninsula is connected to Ukraine in the north by the Isthmus of Perekop, a thin strip of earth that is between five and seven kilometres wide, depending on the location. In the east it is separated from Russia by the Kerch Strait, between three and thirteen kilometres wide. In 1954, for the tricentenary of the Russian-Ukrainian union, the Soviet powers offered Crimea as a present to the Soviet Socialist Republic of Ukraine. The decision, essentially administrative, was taken "in consideration of the economic integration, the territorial proximity, and the economic and cultural bonds"[2] between the peninsula and Ukraine. Before that, for a hundred and eighty years, Crimea was part of Russia. Empress Catherine II had conquered it during a war with the Ottoman Empire, which had held sway over the peninsula for three and a half centuries. Before the Turks, there had been the Greeks. And before the Greeks, many other peoples. In

---

[2] Edict of the Presidium of the USSR Supreme Soviet, February 19, 1954.

the middle of the nineteenth century, the French and the British had come to fight at the side of the Ottomans who were trying to reconquer their peninsula. A few hundreds of thousands of dead later, the three allies won the war, but Crimea remained Russian.

All that is to say that many people died in combat over the centuries, fighting over this strategic appendix on the Black Sea.

When the Soviet Union was disbanded in 1991, Crimea automatically became a region of independent Ukraine. And this, even though part of its population, probably a majority, considered itself Russian. Not only Russian-speaking, but Russian. Russia was the motherland. If the Crimeans at that point had been given the choice of joining Russia or Ukraine, there is a good chance that they would have opted for the former. Nevertheless, there was a community in Crimea that rejoiced at no longer having to deal with Moscow: the Tatars. At the end of the Second World War, Stalin had deported them to central Asia in freight cars, accusing them of having collaborated with the Nazis. They'd only been able to return to their homeland during the 1980s, and they surged back by the tens of thousands. An independent Ukraine was the best they could hope for, and Russia, the worst.

Regardless of the wishes on the one hand or the other, the dismantling of the empire took place behind closed doors. It was left to a handful of men to determine the fate of millions of others. Their decisions were not flawless, but they tried as best as they could to reduce to a minimum the consequences of a process with extremely explosive potential. Things had to be kept simple. And the simplest solution was for the fifteen Soviet republics to become fifteen independent states, while conserving their administrative frontiers.

The Crimeans did not complain too strongly at that point. They diffidently proclaimed the sovereignty of their autonomous republic, while making it clear that they remained an integral part of Ukraine. Their moderation enabled them to negotiate this period of uncertainty quite well. And it left them in much better shape, in any case, than the Chechens, the Transnistrians, and the Abkhazians for example, who tried to redesign the post-Soviet frontiers at the cost of thousands of dead, wounded, and displaced. And so a peaceful Crimea remained the preferred holiday destination for Russians, Ukrainians, and other subjects of the former empire.

During the first two decades under an independent Ukraine, a few Crimean and Russian politicians tried as best they could to wrest the peninsula from Kyiv and to root it in Moscow. But there was no way. The Ukrainian constitution made no provision for its component parts to secede, and Russia was committed to not calling into question the inherited frontiers of the USSR. Whatever the Crimeans might think, the status quo was better for all concerned.

You will forgive me this lengthy introduction to such a small strip of land. It's just that history, as raw material, is very malleable, and you have to move in very close to see how each person can play at manipulating the elements to produce a version that serves his or her interests.

***

The very day that President Yanukovych leaves Kyiv, never to return, a man arrives in Crimea. He speaks calmly, with no emotion. He is forty-three years old, with a greying moustache and hair. He has come from Moscow. Who has sent him? Is he on an official mission for the Russian secret service? Or has he come on his own initiative? He doesn't say. "I tell the truth or else remain silent"[3] is his motto. For the moment, he prefers to remain discrete. He will only appear in public two months later, 650 kilometres from there, not very far from you, as the commander in chief of a rebel group. He will then introduce himself to a journalist of *Komsomolskaya Pravda* under his nom de guerre, Igor "Strelkov," the "sniper."

Igor Girkin - that's his real name - loves history. In peacetime, he participated in the re-enactment of the great battles of the Russian Civil War. In university, he planned for a career as a historian. But rather than contenting himself with studying history, he decided to write it.

On June 25, 1992, the young Igor completed his studies at the Moscow State Institute of History and Archives. The next day, he climbed aboard a train for Tiraspol. The USSR had just fallen apart. Russian speakers from the

---

[3] Interview with the Russian news site, *Svobodnaya Pressa*, November 11, 2014.

region of Transnistria, in Moldava, were waging a secessionist insurrection. Igor went to lend them his support. Not just for the excitement, and even less for money. He was in Transnistria to promote an idea. Igor was a monarchist, he wanted to revive the Czarist Russian Empire. He looked at nineteenth century maps, and dreamed of a Europe divided up as it was at that time.

The Transnistrian separatists proclaimed victory a month after his arrival. Too soon for him. He'd developed a liking for combat. He shifted his gaze to Yugoslavia, which had also just imploded. Along with his Russian comrades, he joined the Serb militia to fight the Bosnian Muslims. He was in the Balkans to defend pan-Slavism, the unity of the Orthodox Slavs, an outgrowth of his imperialist dream. Returning to Russia, he joined the security services. He wanted to continue serving the Russian cause. In the Caucasus, the Chechens had taken up arms to win their independence from Moscow. Great Russia was about to lose one of its territories. Twice, in less than a decade, he helped to crush the Chechen rebels.

It's with this military baggage, this vision of the world, and his warrior's fervour, that Strelkov arrives in Crimea on that February 21, 2014. He sees a historic moment on the horizon; an opportunity to exploit confusion to realize a mad dream. In a few hours, a "fascist junta" will take power in Kyiv following a "coup d'état." The Crimeans will be frightened. They will seek help. Strelkov will work to save them and to bring them home to an imperial Great Russia.

FOR WANT OF A FIR TREE

***

In Simferopol, the Crimean capital, the Kyiv revolution has triggered warring demonstrations. The Russian Crimeans take to the street to reject, loud and clear, the new "fascist" government. The Tatars come out as well, brandishing Ukrainian flags in support of the new powers that be.

In the days following Yanukovych's flight, men in battledress appear like magic in the peninsula's streets. They are hooded, heavily armed, and wear no insignia. They present themselves initially as members of a citizens' self-defence militia newly formed by a few pro-Russia Crimeans. But the lie fools no one. These "little green men," as they're soon called, are too well equipped to be only local volunteers. All it takes is a little urging from behind a camera for one of them to reveal what everyone has already guessed: "We are Russian soldiers, and we have come to prevent terrorist acts."[4]

There it is. Great Russia has decided to make its move. It will not officially acknowledge it until much later, but it has just launched an operation to "save" Crimea and, above all, its own military interests. Was it Igor Strelkov who urged them to intervene, as he will later claim? Or was he not from the outset just carrying out orders from the Kremlin? Only those privy to the secrets of the gods know the answer. In any case, the deployment of the

---

[4] Interview with an anonymous Russian soldier, from the Ukrainian site UkrStream TV, March 4, 2014.

Russian forces is child's play: more than fifteen thousand soldiers are already posted in normal times at the Sebastopol naval base, at the southern end of the peninsula. Reinforcements only have to cross the Kerch Strait to complete the occupation. Within a few hours, the little green men have installed roadblocks at the four corners of Crimea, isolating it from the rest of Ukraine. The Ukrainian soldiers remain in their barracks. They have not received orders from the new government. During this time, Strelkov allies himself with an obscure deputy with a mafia past. Their interests coincide. Sergey Aksyonov will be the inside man, the pseudo-legal face of the operation as it unfolds. Strelkov will stay in the shadows. Now that the clashes on the Maidan have made violence an acceptable political weapon, now that the Ukrainian constitution has been flouted by the "junta," and that the Russian language is in the process of losing its minimal official status, Strelkov, like the Kremlin, calculates that an offensive action will appear to be a legitimate defence.

★★★

On Thursday, February 27, at dawn, a commando group invades the Crimean parliament. Igor Strelkov is at its head. A special session is being held behind closed doors. An undetermined number of deputies elect - voluntarily or by coercion - a new government. The obscure deputy Aksyonov becomes prime minister. The parliamentarians vote to hold a referendum on self-determination.

The powers in Kyiv are concerned, but do not know how to react. In the days that follow, the "polite people" (the other nickname for the little green men), neutralize the Ukrainian military. No need to open fire. The helpless soldiers have still received no orders to defend themselves. They capitulate, one unit at a time. Igor Strelkov negotiates surrenders and defections. In what capacity? It remains a mystery. He persuades generals and hundreds of soldiers to join the Russian forces.

The referendum is moved up a first, then a second time. Everything must be settled as soon as possible, before Kyiv can pull itself together and muster an adequate response to the developments on the peninsula. The referendum question is modified on the run: supporters of the status quo will have no square to tick off. The Crimeans will have to choose between a union with Russia or the demand for even greater autonomy within Ukraine. The "choice" posted on the placards during the lightning campaign leaves no room for nuance:

ON MARCH 16, WE CHOOSE BETWEEN A FASCIST CRIMEA AND A RUSSIAN CRIMEA

The result is as unanimous as it is suspect. According to official figures, 97 per cent of the electorate votes for union with Russia. The voter turnout is more than 80 per cent.

The confusion in Kyiv provided the opportunity to violate the constitution, and then to claim that this violation was no worse than that committed by the revolutionaries. For Moscow and Strelkov, you had to seize the moment: to make the last remnant of the "Russian World" your own before the Ukrainian powers could lay the foundation for a pro-European Ukraine, certain to be anti-Russian. They had to "reunite" Crimea and Russia, even if it meant holding a gun to the temples of those they were coming to free.

Two days later, the Russian parliament ratifies the annexation. Only one of the 444 deputies in the Duma votes against it. All of Russia celebrates.

"*Krym Nash!*"

"Crimea is ours!"

Several diehard opponents of Vladimir Putin, on that day, praise the president's "courage." His popularity reaches heights unequalled during his fourteen years of power. There's nothing like a conquest to make an imperialist nation's hearts beat as one. In Kyiv, and elsewhere in Ukraine, politicians, revolutionaries, and ordinary citizens are dismayed by this amputation of the peninsula. A foreign army that is much more powerful and organized guarantees that no turning back is possible. The border has shifted. The Isthmus of Perekop has closed. A bridge will be built over the Kerch Strait to link Crimea with Russia. Ukraine will have to live with a phantom limb.

★★★

And so, is Crimea a Russian or a Ukrainian territory? Who is right?

You've got the gist, Tyoma, even a deep immersion in history can't help us come up with a fair, indisputable, and definitive answer to this question. When Vladimir Putin says that this territory "has historically been part of Russia," and that he has repaired a "historical injustice"[5] in annexing it, he is selecting bits and pieces from the past that are convenient for him. Using the same argument, the Turks could just as easily claim the same territory, which was in fact under their control for a longer period of time. And why not the Greeks, while we're at it? What criteria determine whether a conquest has become a historical reparation?

For its part, Ukraine demands an end to the "Russian occupation" of *its* Crimea, citing a country's right to its territorial integrity. But what about the internationally recognized right for peoples' self-determination? Do Crimeans of all origins constitute a people entitled to decide on a common future, or are they several little peoples, or are they a part, rather, of one of the great neighbouring nations? Depending on the circumstances, is it their Russian past, their Ukrainian present, or the will of the majority that ought to determine to which nation they belong?

These are complicated questions, I know. But what we ought to remember is that when men say they've con-

---

[5] A speech before the members of the Duma and the Federation Council, March 18, 2014.

quered a territory in order to right a historical injustice, they're probably perpetrating another one just as great. And when their adversaries have as their principal argument laws or treaties to convince you of their indisputable right to a piece of land, they necessarily neglect to take into consideration the willingness of those who live there to share a country with them.

Without the revolution in Kyiv, the Crimeans would probably not have sought to separate from Ukraine. It's even less likely that Russia would have dared to annex a territory it had never officially claimed since the end of the Soviet Union. The historic opportunity to profit from Ukraine's troubles presented itself. Russia and the pro-Russian Crimeans seized it.

★★★

The only thing that can console us in this entire tale, Tyomochka, is that in contrast to the revolution, this amputation without the benefit of anaesthesia took place with almost no shedding of blood. Those four turbulent weeks cost only one life, that of a Ukrainian soldier. Already one too many, it's true. Yet the rapid unfolding of the crisis did not prevent the violence from making inroads into your country. On the contrary. For some it raised hopes of seeing the Crimean scenario repeat itself just as easily in their own region, and with as much fervour on the part both of the population and the invader.

While all might have ended there, Ukraine's descent into chaos had only just begun.

For want of unity, the peninsula was lost.

Chapter 5

THE EAST

Even if *they* had the courage to come before your grave and explain to you why you are dead, I doubt whether they'd be brave enough to tell you the truth. They would say that the war was inevitable, that the Other forced them to take up arms. They'd assure you that they did all they could to protect you, but that the Other wanted your life. And they would swear to avenge your death the only way they know: by defeating the Other, and emerging victorious from this war.

They're lying, of course. They're lying *to themselves*, consciously or not, obsessed as they are by the justice of their cause. The war was avoidable. War is always avoidable. It so happens that the sacrifices and concessions required to forestall it are so hard to swallow that open conflict seems the least terrible of solutions. When social peace feels every day like torture, oppression, and the absence of freedom, it's understandable that a people at the end of its tether can take to the street to drive out a dictatorial regime that does not allow it to do so at the ballot box. It does not want war. It obtains it despite itself. It hopes, naively, that the regime will abdicate in the face of the popular will. But rapidly, the better life on the horizon is replaced by bombs, dead bodies, and refugee camps. The fighters who were supposed to free the people from oppression become oppressors themselves, often worse than the regime in place. The people come to miss the peace they knew and their onetime executioner. That, today's Syrians and Libyans will explain to you better than I possibly can.

Where you live, the war could have been prevented much more easily than under those dictatorships. The price to pay for peace would not have been as steep as the oppression of the weaker by the stronger, nor the unilateral secession of Donbas. Even after the revolution and the Crimean crisis, an accommodation would have been possible.

No hand reached out.

I know perfectly well that "ifs" can never rewrite the past. But to note the lost opportunities is all that remains to us, now that it's too late and that you're six feet underground; all that's left is to hope that one day *they* will stop adding to their accusations and their crimes, including your death, that they will envisage the end of the war, and perhaps, if a bit of humanity remains to them, reconciliation.

★★★

I've already told you that a good number of the Russian-speaking Ukrainians did not support the revolution in Kyiv. The assumption of power by the new government frightened them. The parliamentary vote on the abrogation of the regional languages statute confirmed their fears. Even though the interim president refused to ratify this decision, that didn't stop them from concluding that the nationalists' first reflex was to punish them. The spectre of a new chastisement still hovered over their heads.

In the Russian-speaking regions, the overthrow of Yanukovych swells the size of the anti-Maidan demonstrations. The supporters of the fallen president no longer have to be paid to flock into the streets. Rightly or wrongly, they feel that they must defend their rights, in opposition to the new regime.

During the entire month of March, 2014, in different cities, citizens succeed in taking over local government buildings. Each time, they climb onto the roof and replace the Ukrainian flag with the Russian tricolour. Some of the occupiers urge their region's secession, and its annexation to Russia. Others simply want a decentralization of Ukraine, which would take the form of a federation. The sieges only last for a few hours, after which the Ukrainian security forces expel the protesters. The Ukrainian flag is raised once more. But a few days later, relentlessly, the militants return in greater numbers and retake the building.

At first, these events take place in parallel with those in Crimea. When the Russian troops invade the peninsula and it is united with Russia, the protesters in the east have reason to celebrate. Those who dream of becoming one with Russia can now hope for a similar action on the part of the Russian army where they live. The others, who demand a guarantee that their rights will be protected under the post-revolutionary regime, now have a threat to hold over the revolutionaries' heads. Surely, they say to themselves, the new authorities will want to avoid a repetition of the Crimean scenario.

Their reasoning is logical, but misguided.

Those who took power in Kyiv suffer from a victor's complex. They have no inclination to negotiate with forces resistant to change. The have made the revolution at the cost of a hundred martyrs' blood. They feel that they have won the right to impose their vision of the country. It's for the vanquished to adapt, to join forces with the victors, or to be silent. A corrupt and authoritarian regime has been overthrown; a true democracy, a free and European Ukraine is being born. There will be no compromise with profiteers who have kept the country under the domination of Moscow and brought it to the brink of bankruptcy. Period.

So be it.

But in that case, the anti-Maidans will make no compromises on their own turf. They are many, perhaps even a majority in their regions. If this new Ukraine doesn't want to make a place for them, why should they remain part of it?

On April 6, 2014, three weeks after the annexation of Crimea and six after the revolution, armed militants again advance on the government buildings of Donetsk, Luhansk, and Kharkiv.

In Donetsk, they succeed in maintaining control of the regional headquarters, and the next day proclaim the Donetsk People's Republic (DPR). The powers that be in Kyiv are vaguely concerned, but no more. How could a handful of militants occupying a single building, in a city with a population of one million, constitute a threat to the stability of the country? The Interior Minister makes assurances that that the separatist problem will be resolved within 48 hours, through dialogue or by force. Now, he knows very well that repression is a risky business. The loyalty of the police and the military is too fragile for him to give the order to act. Besides which, a blood bath would turn the local population against the authorities for good. As for dialogue, the Ukrainian prime minister travels to Donetsk four days after the proclamation of the DPR. Since assuming his post two months earlier, it's the first time that Arseniy Yatsenyuk has deigned to visit Donbas. He feels that there are more urgent problems to deal with in Kyiv. And if he now makes the trip, it's not to negotiate with the troublemakers. After all, do they not control just one ordinary building in Donetsk? Yatsenyuk is content just to talk things over with the regional leaders who support him and tell him what he wants to hear: everything will fall into place. The prime minister promises the people of Donbas that the new Ukrainian constitution will be written in concert with them. Then he leaves for Kyiv. He will never return.

★★★

Let us now return to Igor Strelkov in Simferopol. While the grumbling increases in Donbas, he is savouring his victory. Crimea has become Russian once again! As the days pass, he receives many visitors from different Russian-speaking cities in Ukraine: politicians, soldiers, bandits, businessmen, leaders of clandestine organizations, etc. They all make the same appeal: "Come do for us what you did in Crimea." Those who know him also know that this is an offer that Strelkov cannot refuse. For him Ukraine, the state, is an aberration. The south and east of the country are parts of *Novorossiya*, the "New Russia" conquered by Catherine II in the eighteenth century, sadly separated from the mother country by the vagaries of history. Kyiv is still on the ropes. Those newly in power have not yet absorbed the shock of losing the peninsula. The loyalty of the citizens and forces of order in the regions is not at all guaranteed. It's clear that the time is right for another offensive action.

Strelkov succeeds in putting together a commando of fifty-two men. It includes ex-members of the anti-riot forces who fled Kyiv when Yanukovych abandoned them. There are also former soldiers in the Ukrainian army and a few of Strelkov's Russian compatriots. But how, with only fifty-two men, to launch an insurrection whose goal is to take control of territories with millions of inhabitants? The initial target is crucial: a city large enough for the conquest to be a significant one, but small enough for the mission to be accomplished with a commando group of that size. That is how, "completely by chance,"[6] according to Strelkov, Sloviansk is chosen, about a hundred kilometres north of where you live. This city of 120,000 inhabitants has, it seems, good potential for an uprising. And so Sloviansk will be the one. It will become the epicentre for the counter-revolution.

The very day that the Ukrainian prime minister leaves Donetsk after having made some vague promises, Strelkov and his men cross the Russo-Ukrainian border. Once in Sloviansk, they're greeted by about two hundred men from nearby, ready to join them. Without meeting any resistance, they take control of the city's police headquarters, laying their hands on an arsenal of pistols and machine guns. They then take over the security services' building, and that of the municipal government. The police, special agents, bureaucrats, and even the mayor of the city, rally to the rebels.

"They have come to defend our rights!"

Within a few hours, the commando has taken total control of Sloviansk. Roadblocks are set up at strategic points. The next day, it's the neighbouring city of Kramatorsk that falls to them.

---

[6] Interview with the Russian nationalist newspaper *Zavtra*, November 10, 2014.

The pattern has been established. All you have to do is to move in, unannounced, on a city where the new government is unpopular, rally the support of those who exercise state control, gather up the arms and munitions in their reserves, take over the institutions, convert their leaders and get rid of the sceptics, then surround the city to monitor the comings and goings.

If nothing stops Strelkov, soon the whole region will be in his hands.

Meanwhile, in Donetsk, Luhansk, and elsewhere in Donbas, the popular uprisings become more and more serious. Militants become militias. They form battalions, recruit volunteers, seize arms from police arsenals, and set up roadblocks. The rebellion is no longer the bad joke Kyiv thought it was. It's an armed counter-revolution. The interim president has to decree the beginning of an "anti-terrorist operation" in the east. The army launches a timid counter-offensive. It succeeds in regaining control of certain towns. But the rebels are claiming more and more victories. Leaders of the movement are emerging. The uprisings, relatively independent of one another at the beginning, are better and better coordinated. The People's Republic of Donetsk exists beyond the walls of a single building. At the end of April, it's the turn of the Luhansk People's Republic to see the light of day.

The conflict continues to spread. Kyiv cannot believe what is happening. Its soldiers are being ambushed. There are dead. The rebels have the advantage of surprise. It's then that the Maidan revolutionaries really begin to worry.

They see their dream crumbling. If nothing is done, they say to themselves, after Crimea now the entire east will be gobbled up by Russia. They realize that the army, corrupt, poorly trained and equipped, cannot hold back the threat. Not counting the fact that the soldiers' loyalty is suspect. At any moment, entire units could defect and join the enemy, as was the case in Crimea. You can't trust them to save the country. On the Maidan, many revolutionaries have learned to fight. Some have even given their lives for a new Ukraine. Hundreds of others are ready to risk theirs. They're forming battalions, taking up arms, and heading for Donbas without asking the government's permission. As of that moment, it's not two regular armies that are confronting each other, but citizens of the same country who are killing each other because they have a different conception of the state in which they want to live.

Ukraine is in the midst of a civil war.

Soon, bombs will come to replace bullets. The small number of dead will become a few dozen, then a few hundred and a few thousand.

***

The revolutionaries will tell you that this is not a civil war, but purely and simply a foreign invasion aiming to destabilize Ukraine and punish it for having wanted to free itself from the Russian yoke. They will say that after Crimea, the goal of their powerful neighbour is to annex even more territories belonging to its former vassal. They will assure you that the problem is almost wholly external, the proof being that only a handful of local bandits took up arms to support the invader. They will reject any link between the wildfire in Donbas and a certain contempt of the post-revolutionary powers for the residents of a region that was the homeland of the deposed president.

It is perhaps the Russian citizen Igor "Strelkov" Girkin, indeed, who "pressed the trigger to start the war,"[7] as he himself boasts. It's possible that, without the involvement of his commando, the isolated revolts would sooner or later have been checkmated by the army. Strelkov probably doesn't tell the whole truth when he asserts that he initiated his operation in Sloviansk with no support from the Kremlin. It is conceivable that he obtained its tacit agreement at least, or even a promise of support. And perhaps Russia sent reinforcements for the rebellion from the very start and not four months later, as Strelkov swears. I would be lying to you if I claimed to have knowledge of all the behind-the-scenes machinations that led to such a widespread conflict. I'm only an observer who is trying to discern a logic behind each player's actions. The only reason for which you should listen to me rather than those who *know*, is because, unlike them, I'm not trying to defend the righteousness of any cause. What matters to me is to understand and to explain to you why a conflict that could have remained political and unarmed, ended up delivering a rocket to your head.

---

[7] Ibid.

★★★

When the separatists organized their referendums on the sovereignty of their "peoples' republics" in May, barely a month after the start of their rebellion, Vladimir Putin told them that the exercise was pointlessly hasty, and that it should be postponed. Which ought to have made clear to you:

that what was good for Crimea yesterday is not good for you today;

that although you are "historically," perhaps, part of the "Russian World," the fact is that despite these fine words, to annex you would not be in our interests;

yes, we will give moral support to your struggle, and allow our citizens who so desire to go and fight for your cause (this Strelkov, for example);

but don't fool yourselves: we're not doing that because of your pretty face. You're destabilizing Ukraine, and that serves our interests. The day when the nationalists in Kyiv will have understood that they must agree to become partners with us once more if they want to regain their stability, on that day, you'll have to get along on your own;

forget Great Russia and its so-called responsibility for all the Russians outside its borders. This is historical gruel to feed the chauvinist masses. It's a way of lending a semblance of legitimacy to actions whose purpose is to defend our strategic interests, interests that would be otherwise unjustifiable.

That's the word you must retain.
Interests.

***

Without Russia's help, the rebels would have had trouble resisting the Ukrainian forces for more than a few weeks. But without substantial support from the local population, the rebellion would never have taken root in Donbas.

The post-revolutionary powers in Kyiv have every right not to admit their responsibility, partial at least, for the outbreak of war. They can put all the blame on "Russian aggression," and deny that certain of its citizens might have felt excluded following the Revolution of Dignity. But that will do nothing, in retrospect, to prevent the revolt from having erupted, and spread.

And that does not change the fact either, Tyomchik, that as of the moment that the war settles in, your days are numbered.

For want of the peninsula, the east was lost.

PART II

DIRTY WAR

*For want of the east,
thousands of lives were lost.*

Chapter 1

TOUCHING DOWN

When I arrive in Ukraine, on January 7, 2015, you have only eleven days to live.

I've missed the revolution, the amputation of Crimea, and the first nine months of the war in Donbas. Since the beginning of December, a truce between the rebels and the Ukrainian forces has reduced the fighting considerably. It sometimes happens that one or two soldiers are mowed down by a shell, but civilians have stopped dying. However, truce is not a synonym for peace. It's a reprieve that keeps alive a faint hope for peace, most often in vain. With the holiday season coming to an end, a renewal of hostilities, sooner or later, is a real possibility, not unwelcome to the people with arms, and above all those who lead them. The rebels claim thousands of square kilometres beyond those they control. The Ukrainian forces swear that they will not rest as long as the territories they have lost have not been reconquered. Russia, for its part, continues to deny any involvement in the conflict. But for a long time it has not been able to hide the fact that it has been furnishing soldiers and arms to support the rebels. For her, this war is a thorn in the side of Kyiv's post-revolutionary government. As long as it will seek to turn away from her, to join NATO and the European Union, Russia will continue to fuel the rebellion.

In the plane, the newspapers talk more about Syria and Nigeria than of Donbas. There I read, notably, that during the year 2014, which has just ended, 11,245 people were killed in violent clashes between the Nigerian army and the jihadists of Boko Haram. That's many more than here, where the war has made 4,700 victims. 4,700 too many. I will spare you the count from Syria, where the dead have long been counted in the tens of thousands.

That will perhaps seem strange to you, Tyoma, but even before arriving in Ukraine, I cannot prevent myself from placing this conflict in perspective, looking at it in the context of all the others. You are not yet dead, but I am thinking of those countless innocents who will also lose their lives elsewhere under circumstances that are equally unjust. Why should your funeral merit the meagre editorial space I'll be able to wrest from a few media outlets, more than that of Mohammed, assassinated by Islamist insurgents in Aleppo in Syria, or that of Ayeesha, killed by an American drone in Tappi, Pakistan? Why should Ukraine receive more of our attention than Yemen, the Central African Republic, or the Congo? And why those wars rather than the silent dramas - famines, epidemics, droughts - that kill as many or more, far from the great geopolitical arenas? The truth is that there is no good reason. The coverage of the great and small events that shape our world is an inexact science, arbitrary and unfair. There is no flawless mathematical calculation that enables us to classify tragedies according to their seriousness or importance, so as to determine which are the most deserving of our attention.

My own justifications for coming to cover the conflict in Ukraine are arbitrary: I speak Russian, but not Arabic, Hausa, or Pashtun. I am familiar with Ukraine, Russia, the post-Soviet lands, and so can claim a certain authority when I try to explain the roots and consequences of this conflict. I pay for my own travels, and I know that in Ukraine I have a better chance of recouping my investment than elsewhere, and even reaping a certain profit. And there is the matter of security. In a time of urban guerrillas and terrorist movements, when all the laws of war have been shot to pieces, the conflict in your country has remained, all things considered, conventional. The front line is fairly clear. It separates two armed groups, relatively symmetrical in their organization and the methods they employ. Foreign journalists are not targets for either side. No one is trying to kidnap them and hold them for ransom, or to cut their throats in front of a camera and then post the video on YouTube for the purposes of promotion and recruitment. Foreign journalists (it's more complicated for those who are Russian and Ukrainian) work on both sides of the trenches with more or less the same access and the same restrictions. In short, aside from the bombs that can fall at any time and anywhere - you know that better than I do - the dangers in Donbas remain circumscribed.

FOR WANT OF A FIR TREE

I am not a war reporter. I do not want to be a war reporter. War repels me. I do not want to have anything to do with this romantic aura that surrounds those who cover destruction and death, risking their lives and their mental health. I do not seek to become a legend or a martyr of journalism.

I tell you all that, and at the same time I find myself in an airplane on my way to cover a war. It's that despite everything, despite this fear of death that has held me in its grip since childhood, perhaps even because of that, I cannot stop myself from *going to see what must be seen*. I am trying my best to assess the dangers, hoping that when the moment comes, I will be able to resist the temptation to cross my own red lines.

Chapter 2

KYIV, POST-REVOLUTION

It's the night of Orthodox Christmas. In the subway, young people are singing traditional hymns. The Ukrainian girls are as beautiful as always. The boys, just as curt, just as brash. The fare is still two hryvnias, just as it was during my last visit five years earlier to cover Yanukovych's election. No one has since had the political nerve to raise it. At the time, the American dollar was worth five hryvnias. It's now worth sixteen.

Coming out of the subway, I find myself on the Maidan. At first, the square seems intact, as if it had never been the theatre of a bloody revolution that had disfigured it. New bricks have replaced the old, prised up by the demonstrators to build barricades or serve as projectiles to be launched against the security forces. But taking a closer look, I see traces of the recent past. The post office columns are still daubed with the demonstrators' slogans. There's a bulletin board covered with photographs of people who vanished during the revolution, along with notes outlining the circumstances of their disappearance. Some are overlaid with the word "Found," with no more details. Did they reappear dead or alive? The Trade Unions Building next to the Maidan is hidden by a huge banner, on which you can read "Glory to Ukraine! To the heroes, glory!" against the background of a bright yellow wheat field and a dazzling blue sky split at the horizon to reproduce the bicoloured Ukrainian flag. The building, which was one of the headquarters of the demonstrators during the Euromaidan, burned down at the height of the clashes. On the other side of the square, a minibus offers passers-by an excursion to Mezhyhirya, to see the sumptuous residence of the former President Yanukovych, overrun by protesters after his flight. At the foot of a statue of the goddess Berehynia, a photo exhibition recounts the highlights of the revolution. Among the images of the heroic demonstrations and the fierce combats, I find a few showing the skeleton of the controversial New Year's fir tree, garlanded with revolutionary posters:

The vegetable is ripe, it's time to throw it out!
Long live Free Ukraine! No to political repression!
Russia, arise! Putler,[8] out!

This year, there is no fir tree on the Maidan. The municipal authorities have decided that it would be indecent, if not dangerous, to erect one. What with the war in Donbas and the disenchantment of many with regard to those in power, a new wave of mass protests in Kyiv cannot be ruled out.

On the edge of the square, on Institutska Street, a low wall has been transformed into a pantheon of the "Heav-

---

[8] A conflation of Putin and Hitler.

enly Hundred." The portraits of each of the hundred and two men and three women killed during the revolution have been placed in a separate section, garlanded with lanterns, flowers, and little flags.

On top of the hill, still on Institutska, relics of those tragic days are scattered pell-mell where demonstrators perished beneath the bullets while trying to breach the doors of the presidential headquarters: paving stones, wooden or iron shields, orange miners' helmets, gas masks, wooden cudgels and swords, improvised pieces of armour, prayer sheets, etc. Everything, everywhere, celebrates their sacrifice. For obvious reasons, on the other hand, nowhere do you find the weapons and likenesses of the eighteen policemen who died defending another idea of Ukraine. The winners have written the history, have chosen their heroes.

★★★

Among the commemorative alcoves, I spot the one honouring Viktor Khomiak. In the photo, you see him with a timid smile, holding an enormous fish in his two hands. The caption below describes him as a fifty-four-year-old "social activist" from the region of Volyn in the west of the country. I'd read about him before coming to Ukraine. His story intrigued me, especially because it was related to that cursed New Year's fir tree.

How did Viktor Khomiak come to be one of the Revolution of Dignity's immortals?

FOR WANT OF A FIR TREE

On January 27, 2014, around eleven o'clock in the morning, a demonstrator on the Maidan spots a silhouette swaying inside the metal structure of the fir tree. It can barely be seen behind the many posters that have been plastered there over the recent weeks. It's a dead body. How has it ended up there without anyone noticing, when the encampment around it is swarming with demonstrators all day and all night? Strange.

The police come to take down the corpse. The autopsy reveals no sign of violence. The authorities conclude that it's a suicide. Would Viktor Khomiak have had the perverse idea of taking his own life just as one's hopes for a better future seemed no longer futile? Bizarre.

On the Maidan, no one remembers Viktor. Yet he was camping there for two months. In fact, it's the events surrounding the erection of the fir tree that made him decide, at the beginning of December, to leave his village and to join the protesters. If truth be told, he hadn't much else to do with his life. In the autumn, he'd lost his job in a factory. He was living with his old mother and his daughter, already an adult. His wife had left him for another man several years earlier.

Three hours before his death, Viktor had talked with his daughter. He'd told her about standing guard the previous night at the Trade Unions Building. He'd said that he was exhausted and was going to lie down in the encampment. Nothing in his voice or what he said suggested that he was going to end his days.

When it receives his body, his family observes that it bears several marks of violence: wounds to the head, nails ripped out, abrasions on the hands. Nothing like the official autopsy. Had Viktor then "been suicided"? Then how would the murderers have been able to infiltrate the square with the body and hang it inside the fir tree without being noticed? Unless the torture session had taken place inside a tent on the Maidan?

The plot thickens.

At the time when Viktor's death is taking place, the protesters have other concerns. They have just seen their first comrades fall under police gunfire. They have a regime to overthrow. Solving the mystery of the hanged man is not their priority. As for the authorities, they only have limited access to the scene of the crime, which is under the control of the demonstrators. In any case, they are suspected of being responsible for the murder. It's hard to imagine an objective investigation under those circumstances.

Days pass. The confrontations on the Maidan become more and more violent. There are more and more victims. The affair of the hanged man is buried a bit deeper every day beneath the historical developments and the dramas. Less than a month after Viktor's death, the demonstrators celebrate their victory. The chiefs of police are replaced by new ones, sympathetic to the revolution. Despite that, the Khomiak affair is not reopened. Viktor is now just one dead man among others.

When the revolutionaries later constitute their pantheon, they compile a register of all the Maidan victims. Viktor Khomiak died on the Maidan. He was a demonstrator. He is automatically included in the list, and receives the title Hero of Ukraine.

Viktor was perhaps killed for his ideas, for wanting to build a new Ukraine. It is also possible that his death had nothing to do with the events of the day. Perhaps he committed suicide for reasons he carried with him to his grave. Unless there's a story of an unpaid debt that cost him his life, or some other unrelated murky business? Today, the truth interests no one. Viktor's family received the honours and rewards due them for his presumed sacrifice. The Euromaidan has one more martyr to justify the toppling of the old regime.

Viktor is a hero. A collateral hero of the revolution.

★★★

As you can see, Artyom, the Maidan, that heart of the country where the moods of the people are made manifest, has a lot to say about the revolution it saw unfold on its paving stones the previous year. On the other hand, it says almost nothing about the war still being waged where you lived. There are of course some volunteers who criss-cross the square, moneyboxes around their necks, collecting donations for the volunteer battalions, but portraits of the "martyrs" of Donbas, fighters or civilians, are nowhere to be found. As of today, however, they would constitute forty-seven additional Heavenly Hundreds. But the capital prefers to hallow the memory of the revolution that gave it back its dignity, rather than to remind us of its more disastrous consequences for the country's unity. In the parliament, in the council of ministers building, in the city hall, in all the administrative buildings a few hundred metres from the Maidan, men and women are in the process of consolidating the ideals of the revolution. They are passing laws, battling corruption, implanting reforms, reinventing the economy, *desovietizing* the country, and *europeanizing* it. The other front, the military front, is hundreds of kilometres away. Seen from here it seems like a virtual war, detached from daily life. A distant disagreement that cannot be dismissed, but that one tries as far as possible to put out of one's mind in order to concentrate on the realization of the dream for which one has fought.

When the Maidan deigns to speak of the war, it's not surprising that it prefers to employ slogans whose opaqueness masks the tragedy lurking behind them.

"Edina kraina. Yedinaya strana."

"A united country." This slogan, in Ukrainian and Russian, dominates the advertising space around Independence Square. There is a dual, hidden irony behind the message. Not only does it declare that this country, facing a separatist rebellion that is threatening its territorial integrity more gravely than anything in its recent history, is "united," but it does so, appending to the official language, unusually, a translation into Russian, the debate over whose status was one of the key factors leading to the outbreak of the war, and to the partition of the country.

A united country? The aspiration is legitimate. The reality is something else entirely.

★★★

One afternoon, I attend a press conference being given by the deputy minister of industry, energy, and coal, at the Ukraina Hotel, facing the Maidan. Yury Zyukov explains to the journalists that two-thirds of the country's coal mines are to be found in the territory occupied by the rebels: "To get through the winter, we must continue to import coal." Before the conflict, not only was Ukraine able to supply all its industries with coal thanks to its own production, but it even managed to export some of it. Today, it must import it from South Africa... and Russia!

Imagine, Artyom.

The nationalists and the pro-Europeans made a revolution in order to get out from under the thumb of their great neighbour. In turn, the neighbour reacted by supporting groups that sought to destabilize the new power. All this led to a separatist conflict that cut Ukraine off from its internal sources of coal. Now, it must import the fuel from Russia in order to keep its metallurgical industry functioning. With the metal that comes out of its foundries, it manufactures weapons that serve to combat the separatists and the Russian soldiers supporting them. On its end, Russia, hit by economic sanctions imposed by Western countries because of its implication in the destabilization of Ukraine, cannot allow itself to refuse the revenue it derives from the exportation of its coal.

You see, when it's a question of money, even the worst of enemies can come to an understanding.

Yuri Zyukov goes on to reel off a series of figures. He talks of the savings achieved since Ukraine has been importing its coal. "It costs less per tonne at today's rate than what we extracted from Donbas before the conflict, and which was heavily subsidized."

Coal, the pride of your region's working class, emblem of its economic power and of its country's distinctive character within the country, a mineral that has sustained families for generations, is, in the end, an industry on life support.

Just one more paradox, you will agree.

The deputy minister now cedes the floor to Andriy Lysenko, spokesperson for the Anti-Terrorist Operation. That's what the Ukrainian authorities call the war in the east. In fact, they never use the term "war." For those in power, Ukraine is not at war. It is fighting terrorists. They know perfectly well that those thousands of Ukrainians who have taken up arms against them do not have as their principal objective to sow terror. But in our day, to attach the label *terrorist* to any dissidence is the best way to demonize it, without having to take into consideration its demands, which are at times legitimate. The revolutionaries cannot be blind to the fact that Yanukovych did the same thing to them in February, 2014. Officially, the bloody confrontation on the Maidan that led to his fall was an anti-terrorist operation against armed demonstrators.

At the microphone, the spokesperson Lysenko declares that in the course of the last twenty-four hours the fighting has intensified in Donbas. Four soldiers have been killed, and eight others wounded. He attributes this rise in tension to the arrival of a Russian "humanitarian convoy" in the region, insinuating that it was transporting munitions rather than blankets and food.

Later in the day, Donetsk's dissident city hall confirms that there are two civilian victims. The first two in a month.

Hostilities have resumed. Just as I'm getting ready to leave for Donbas.

Chapter 3

MEZHYHIRYA

The day before leaving for the east, I make my way to Mezhyhirya, the former residence of Viktor Yanukovych, twenty kilometres north of Kyiv. For years, investigative journalists dreamed of being able to see inside. The president's private life was literally walled off in secrecy. The wildest rumours circulated on the subject.

"They say that the toilet bowls are made of gold!"

Today, anyone can get into Mezhyhirya without risk of breaking a leg and ending up in prison. All you have to do is to buy a 20 hryvnia ticket from the woman at the Corruption Museum's booth, then to present it to the security guard at the sentry box. On weekends, many Kyiv residents come to stroll in family groups through the property's 140 hectares. In so doing they can also enjoy the open air, the greenery, and observe the results of years of public funds being diverted, to the advantage of one man.

In February, 2014, it only took a single revolutionary day for the taxpayers to lay hands on the residence they'd been funding, unknowingly, for much too long a time.

FOR WANT OF A FIR TREE

On this Saturday morning, once it seems clear that the president and his henchmen have flown the coop, hundreds of Maidan demonstrators set off for Mezhyhirya. They enter it without meeting any resistance. They discover a four storey house as kitschy as it is luxurious, a collection of vintage automobiles, a golf course, a heliport, a yacht, rare birds, a kennel of pedigreed dogs, ostriches (!), and much more evidence of the president's extravagant life style. No sign, however, of the notorious golden toilets.

Approaching the Dnieper River, which borders the property, protesters spot boxes of documents drifting to the bottom of the water. They see that some of the files have been partly burned before being tossed in by those hastening away. A few brave souls plunge to retrieve them. Professional divers are called in to help.

Over the following days, dozens of volunteers and journalists work at drying out the documents in the presidential sauna, after which they are photographed and digitized. What is revealed goes beyond their wildest imaginings. The facts are there, black on white, confirmed in the hundreds: bribery, illicit purchases, misappropriation of funds. Everyone knew the president was corrupt.

Now, they have the evidence.

The revolution has a meaning.

The president had to be overthrown.

Yulia Kapitsa arrived at Mezhyhirya on February 23, 2014, the day after its invasion by the protesters. She came directly from the Maidan to help dry out and inventory the compromising documents. Eleven months later, she's still there. She's the one responsible for guiding visitors through the four floors of the Honka, Yanukovych's principal residence, whose nickname derives from the Finnish firm that designed it. During her first days in Mezhyhirya, Yulia was determined to ferret out the truth surrounding the president's embezzlements. What she found was that not everyone had her moral standards. Avarice was trumping ideals. The revolutionaries had become pillagers.

"It saddened me that people did not resist the temptation. I understand that they'd never seen so much luxury in their lives, that they'd lost control and wanted to grab whatever they thought they could resell. But some stole cold-bloodedly. They came prepared. They arrived with tools, presented themselves as former employees come to retrieve their personal effects, and dismantled what they wanted to carry off."

We're in one of the Honka's many rooms. A long sculpted wood table holds pride of place in the middle of the room, surrounded by twelve chairs. Yet the residence was conceived to house only two people, the president and his mistress. (He was living apart from his wife.) Yanukovych did not hold meetings in this house, and invited very few people. Pure extravagance. Yulia points out two wine pitchers on a piece of furniture near the table, sitting on a silver platter. One of the lids has been torn off, probably by the pillagers. "They must have thought it was real gold." It was to swim against this tide and prevent more thefts that Yulia stayed on at Mezhyhirya. Along with the other amateur curator, she helped to save most of the house's paintings. They were sent to the National Art Museum of Ukraine to be safely stored. But many valuable objects, and others of less importance, like the presidential couples' clothes, disappeared in the days following the invasion.

Yulia is here as a volunteer, housed, fed, "compensated," but not really paid. She's had no work since she left her job in a Berdyansk[9] bank to join the Euromaidan in Kyiv. She seems to take no particular pleasure in her current task. Her profile is thin, her gaze is stern, determined, but sometimes exasperated. It's that of a woman of conviction, even stubbornness. That's what it takes to remain here, at the age of thirty-one, rather than to go and remake a post-revolutionary life and career, like the others. With her skills, she could certainly seek an administrative post in the state structure, where she would replace a bureaucrat too closely associated with the former regime. But Yulia feels that it's her duty to stay here, surrounded by luxury, leading an ascetic existence.

On leaving each room in the Honka, Yulia quickly turns out the lights. Everywhere, heating is reduced to a minimum. Ironically, the symbol of Yanukovych's opu-

---

[9] In the southeast of Ukraine.

lence and excess is poor as a church mouse. Only the meagre revenue from the admission tickets is there to support the property. It's because after the revolution, Mezhyhirya found itself in a juridical no man's land. The very day that it was taken over by the protesters, parliament was quick to vote for its nationalization. Since then, the transfer of the property has never been formalized. "The government is afraid to assume its responsibilities," according to Yulia. If it takes over Mezhyhirya, it exposes itself to lawsuits on the part of the official owners, the former president's dummy companies.

"I'm going to stay here for as long as the state does not take possession. I know I'll probably have to wait until the war ends for it to happen, because that's now the main priority. If I'd not been here from the beginning, I probably would not have remained. Now I can no longer leave. Sometimes I have gloomy thoughts. But when people come and are interested in what's happening here, that encourages me. They're thankful that we've conserved all this. I don't want to boast. It happened by chance. I was just there at the right time."

As it happens, a grateful couple from Dnipropetrovsk are taking part in the visit. Natalya Grechanik and her fiancé were curious to see Mezhyhirya during their stay in Kyiv.

"I was pretty sure that our president lived better than ordinary people. But I still thought that there was a bit more equality between our leaders and us. I voted for Yanukovych in the last election. So I'm a bit to blame. We, the people, let that happen. We didn't overthrow him earlier.

"Today many members of my family, friends, colleagues, are leaving the country. Me, I'd like to start a family here, to raise my children in Ukraine. I'm going to stay as long as possible, as long as I haven't exhausted all my options for keeping myself busy. I'm trained as a teacher, but I don't work in that field, because in our country educators are paid miserably.

"I've supported Euromaidan since the beginning. I'm Russian-speaking. Dnipropetrovsk is very near to Donetsk. I don't understand why, in Donbas, some people think that the activists of *Pravy Sektor*[10] are fascists. We never thought that, where we come from. I knew perfectly well that the militants would not shoot all the people who spoke Russian. They're fair-minded. What do I think of Putin and Russia? I'm of two minds on the subject. Before, I was certain that they wanted to conquer Ukrainian territory. But now, there is information that shows... I don't know."

Natalia is confused. She comes from a city where counter-revolutionary tactics have never found much support. A local oligarch even formed his own militia to thwart secessionist plans (and to protect his businesses.) On one side, she's attached to Ukraine. But watching the propaganda on Russian television, she no longer knows who to believe: her government, which also indulges in propaganda, or those who are portrayed as the enemy, but swear that they want to defend Russian-speakers' rights.

---

[10] "The Right Sector," an ultranationalist group born during the Euromaidan.

Natalia's ideas are clouded by the fog of war.

★★★

The guided tour is almost over. Beneath a crystal chandelier, Yulia explains that in her opinion Yanukovych's greatest achievement is the very reason for his fall: "If things turned out as they did, it's because the president was divorced from reality. Living here, he had no need to go anywhere, or to meet ordinary Ukrainians. He had his own medical clinic, his hair salon, a gas station, a cinema, and even a chapel where a priest came to officiate! He was isolated. He got news, but it was filtered. Seen from here, all was going well." I ask Yulia what she thinks of the results of this revolution, with people still waiting for the promised reforms, and war tearing Donbas apart.

"I'm not yet disillusioned with the new government. I didn't expect great reforms, or that in six months we would be part of Europe. I was ready for so many upheavals that nothing surprised me anymore. In fact, the last thing I would have imagined, the worst possible catastrophe on my list, was a war, and it happened. That said, perhaps tomorrow Honka will burn, and me with it. Some hope so. If I seem pessimistic, it's because I came out of the Maidan with a mindset that prevents me from planning anything at all in advance. On the square, you brought food up to the barricades at night, not knowing if the next day there would still be barricades."

Yulia is the embodiment of what the revolution has produced at its best. The movement's detractors can say as much as they want that it was led by a bunch of fascists remote-controlled by foreign governments, but there really were people participating with the noblest of intentions. Of course, incorruptibility, altruism, and asceticism are not for everyone. There are just a few today keeping the revolution afloat in the face of those who want to hijack it for their personal profit. And most of the time, the good side loses.

★★★

At Mezhyhirya, you also find chameleons. Mykola Kashka is one of them. He's fifty-nine years old, and has many gold crowns. His passion, ever since he was knee high to a grasshopper, is pigeons. "Young people are interested in their cell phones, I like pigeons. That's what is most precious to me." When Yanukovych became president, he hired Mykola to take care of his pigeon coop. "He was a true enthusiast like me. He'd had pigeons for forty years." Mykola takes hold of one of the birds, and shows me the band with a Ukrainian flag around its foot. *Viktor Yanukovych, UA*, it reads, in English.

Mykola is not interested in politics. The fall of the president, his boss? "A chair never stays empty for long. Someone leaves, someone else takes his place. That's life. What's important is that things go better, or at least, not worse. Because when things start to go bad, there's no end to it." Mykola is not a man to make waves. He prefers to blend into the background. When I ask him if the situation has improved since the revolution, he describes all the backsliding of the last year. No improvement. Still, he refuses to draw any conclusions. "Before, I earned four thousand hryvnias. I had a workbook, everything was legal. After the revolution, they told me that I could stay as a volunteer for two thousand hryvnias per month." I suspect that Mykola does not want to criticize the new authorities too harshly, for fear of losing his pigeons. Or perhaps it's his Soviet instinct that prevents him from getting mixed up in politics. During the decades of authoritarianism, the least sign of dissidence could cost you your career, or even your life.

Fortunately for Mykola, the revolutionaries need him as much as he needs them. The pigeons were certainly a presidential extravagance, but you couldn't just let them die. Who else but Mykola could deal with them? Who would know how to feed them and take care of them? The pigeon-keeper is no threat to the new power and its reforms. He expresses no particular sympathy for Yanukovych, other than their shared love for the pigeons. Mykola was docile and indispensable. And so he has survived the purges untouched.

The revolutionaries had to face reality: it's not because you turn a country upside down that you can get rid of all the machinery of the former regime from one day to the next.

Chapter 4

THE SOLDIER

The Korean train that runs to Donbas is fast and brand new. It was introduced two years before the onset of the war, just in time for the European football championships. During its first years of use, it covered the 800 kilometres between Kyiv and Donetsk in six hours and forty minutes, almost twice as rapidly as the old Soviet trains. Since the beginning of the war, the trip is shorter. The Intercity does not reach its final destination, where you live. The end point shifts from month to month, depending on the location of the front line.

I stop at Kramatorsk, two stations before the last. You'll remember, it's the second city that Igor Strelkov's commando brought under its control. The Ukrainian army retook it over the summer, and set up the headquarters of its Anti-terrorist Operation (ATO) at the military airfield. I have to go there to pick up my journalistic accreditation. A few days earlier, you could get it in Kyiv. And a few weeks earlier, it didn't exist at all. It's almost the first anniversary of the conflict, but the military bureaucracy is not always up to par. Under those circumstances, nothing is simple.

When I arrive at the roadblock in front of the airfield, the soldiers on guard have no idea of the new procedures. I'm among the first to seek my card here. A polite soldier invites me to make myself at home in the sentry box, while awaiting news from the press centre. He lights the heater, to make sure I don't freeze. The cabin is lined with heart-shaped letters written by children to encourage the soldiers. A collage shows two happy people on a green lawn, surrounded by flowers, a butterfly, a tree, a sun, a cloud, and a Ukrainian flag. *Thank you for Kramatorsk*, the child has written.

Perhaps, Tyomochka, someone at the daycare asked you to do a pretty drawing for the rebel militia on the other side of the front line?

***

One good thing about long waits is that they force you to fill up the time. During the two hours that I spend in the sentry box, I chat on and off with the gentle soldier. He's called Igor. He's forty-six years old, and is retired from the Ukrainian army's special forces. He took part in the Euromaidan, like his comrades keeping guard along with him. Unsurprisingly, when the fighting began in the east, he volunteered to help save his country from the separatist threat. He comes from western Ukraine, but he has a child in Mariupol, a city that the separatists are threatening to attack at any moment.

Even if Kramatorsk is under Ukrainian control, Igor is aware that its population's hearts are still to be won: "Half the people here support the rebels, and a third have family members fighting in their ranks." Recently, a dozen grenade launchers were found in the cemetery a few hundred metres from the airfield. "They're preparing diversionary actions. Not everything is calm in Kramatorsk."

After a moment of silence, I tell him that war, really, is the last thing I would have imagined in Ukraine.

"Ah…"

Somewhere between his sigh and his silence, I feel his heart bleeding. His country in fragments; his uniform once more on his back; risking to kill or to be killed by his compatriots. It's obviously not what he'd foreseen as a plan for the future.

From time to time, Igor turns the dial of one of the old brown military telephones in the sentry box to ask the press centre how my accreditation is coming along. I can't call, myself. The cellular transmissions have been scrambled to prevent the enemy from intercepting exchanges in the area. What is more, I've arrived in the midst of a military exercise. Everything is working slowly.

Outside, the soldiers are having fun with their machine guns. They simulate a shoot-out, making jokes. "You can settle some things with the right words. But with the right words and a pistol, you can settle everything!" one of them exclaims.

Two representatives of a transport company show up at the sentry post. As of today, the Ukrainian military has barred their trucks from travelling between Donetsk and Kramatorsk. "They told us to get a special permit from the ATO's headquarters. That's all we know..." They bring out the documents describing the operations of their company. Igor sighs again, out of discouragement, this time. "Do you know who you're supposed to meet here? Do you have a name, anything?" They have no idea. "The rules change every day," says one of the men. "More like every hour!" replies Igor. It's not just a matter of bureaucratic whims, he explains: "There are enemy spies among us." To avoid its tactics being foiled, the army has to change its codes and rules on a regular basis. Igor works the dial of one of his telephones. He really tries to help the two men, who are seeking a return to the normality and predictability of the pre-war business climate. "They're telling me that you have to go and inquire at the municipal offices." The representatives leave empty-handed.

I offer my analysis of the situation to Igor. It seems to me that the only way to resolve this conflict would be for the Ukrainian president to come to an agreement with his Russian counterpart on a new economic partnership, in exchange for aid to the rebels being suspended. "If Petro Poroshenko signs anything at all with Putin, there will be another Maidan. In any case, if he does that, myself and all the others you see here will go back and demonstrate."

Igor is aware that the Ukrainian army and the volunteer battalions cannot stand up to the rebel forces and the Russian soldiers that support them. "Yes, they're stronger and have greater numbers than we do. But leaving them this territory is not an option. If the Russians left, in two weeks we'd reconquer everything." Exactly, and for that to happen, Russia would have to win some concessions from the new Ukraine, something the revolutionaries such as Igor refuse in principle.

A vicious circle.

Igor sees only one option, to bring things to an end. A great military offensive. "But that won't happen. There would be too many civilian deaths, and too much international attention given to what's going on here, for us to risk it."

He's wrong. In a few days, the Ukrainian army will launch one of those great, merciless offensives. That's what will cost you your life.

Chapter 5

LENINOPAD

Sunday afternoon, the Sloviansk central square. A few dozen citizens are gathered there. In front of them, a five-and-a-half-metre high Lenin gazes into the distance towards the radiant future he'd promised to the proletariat during the October Revolution a century earlier. Someone has hung the the flag of independent Ukraine around his neck as a scarf.

Let us do away with this relic of the totalitarian past! a poster reads.

The Soviet leader has held pride of place in front of the Sloviansk city hall for decades. So many years, during which, in ordinary times, no one paid it any attention. It was part of the landscape. But now, Sloviansk is passing through a period that is anything but ordinary. And old Lenin, suddenly, finds himself once more at the centre of debates concerning the future of the city.

In Sloviansk, people were in large part opposed to the Revolution of Dignity of February, 2014. Enough, at least, for Igor Strelkov to wager that it was the ideal jumping off point for a counter-revolution. Here, like elsewhere in Russian-speaking and industrial Donbas, nostalgia for the Soviet era was strong. Many frowned on the new power's wish to cut all ties with Russia. Their support for Strelkov's commando was motivated by those feelings.[11]

Under the rebels' rule, the separatist and Russian flags flew between the statue and the city hall on the main square.

Lenin, The Peoples' Republic of Donetsk, Russia.

The past, the present, the future.

But since Sloviansk has been retaken by the Ukrainian forces, those who supported the rebels have found themselves on the wrong side of history. Lenin too. And so now it's the European and Ukrainian flags that ripple in the wind in front of the city hall.

Lenin, Ukraine, Europe.

The past, the present, the future.

For most of those who are taking part today in the citizens' meeting, the insurrection has shown that it's urgent business to get rid of the bronze Bolshevik. They must ensure for good and all that his dark legacy does not exert any influence over the present and future of the city. Still, a few nostalgic diehards have dared to turn up and defend their hero in defiance of the dominant mood. The pro- and anti-Lenins take turns at the megaphone. Some in the crowd have their say without having been invited to speak.

---

[11] Paradoxically, the monarchist Igor Strelkov was appalled by the Soviet era. He dreamed of the Russian Empire being reborn, not the USSR.

- Why not sell off the monument, like they've done elsewhere? It's worth 2,800,000 hryvnias!

- Sell it and then steal the money, is that what you want?

- We could replace it with a statue to honour someone who really did something for the city. Lenin never set foot here, or in Ukraine, for that matter!

- But why take it away? It's not hurting anyone, this monument!

- Twenty years ago, the Baltic countries tore down their Lenin statues. Since then, they've been on the path to Europe. As long as this statue stays here, nothing good will happen. It gives the city a bad feeling.

In the crowd, a few scowling old ladies murmur their disapproval. They're soon upbraided. "If you don't like it here, go live in Russia! Or even better, go to Donetsk, it's very nice there, apparently!"

Natalia is a fifty-year-old who's very quick to fire back at the Communist babushkas. I start asking her questions in Russian, the language she used to insult her adversaries. She replies in Ukrainian.

- Can you please answer me in Russian? I don't understand Ukrainian, I say.

- Excuse me. But in Canada, as far as I know, they like Ukraine, so you should know Ukrainian better, no?

- It's just that, you see, I lived in Moscow for a long time, so I speak Russian instead.

- Are you with Russian television?

- Not at all.

- Because I won't give an interview to Russian television.

- I write in French.

A bit reassured, Natalia tells me why she's there for the gathering.

- We want our city to get back control of its own affairs. We want to decide what monuments should be standing on the main square. We're very grateful to the Ukrainian army for having liberated our city. People who supported the invaders don't understand anything about the situation. None of them have very much education. No doctor, no intellectual has joined their movement.

- Do you know people who support the separatists?

- Yes. Some of my neighbours. In fact, I was arguing with them today, about Lenin. I told them that we ought to put him in Lenin Park, which already exists, and they could still go and see him there. Lenin is the symbol of totalitarianism. He's the past. He's not our history. He destroyed the churches. How can he now stand in front of the one right there? I'm not saying we should take radical measures. Half the city is for the statue, the other half is against it. Everyone has the right to their opinion, and you have to take that into consideration. Many have links to Russia. I have family there, myself. But I think it has to be moved. We can deal with our differences in a peaceful manner. I've lived here for thirty years. Before, no one brought up the question of language. I speak Russian and Ukrainian. We've never had any problems on that count. It's Yanukovych who blew things out of proportion, to sow discord. I still wish the daycares would teach our children Ukrainian rather than Russian, like they're doing now. Our young people should know their roots.

- Did you stay here during the insurrection?

- No, we left for Odessa. My husband was sick. He had an open-heart operation. We didn't have to pay anything. The Ukrainian state took care of it all, and we thank it for that. We also left the city because they were bombing. Our neighbour died when a shell fell on his house. A classmate of my daughter was also killed.

- And just who was bombing?

- The bombs that fell on the houses were Russian bombs, launched by the rebels. I can't prove anything, but for the most part they were provocations on their part.

Natalia's pro-Ukrainian profession of faith is absolute. So much so that it seems overblown. Doubtless, she really does support a united Ukraine. But in these troubled times, silent support is not enough. You have to shout it from the rooftops to prove your unfailing loyalty to the forces controlling the city. Especially if you're Russian-speaking, in a divided city. To a journalist, even a foreign one, you must speak Ukrainian.

★★★

Since the fir tree incident on the Maidan, hundreds of Lenins have been taken down across the country. But hundreds of others are still there in plain sight on the main squares. The debates surrounding their fate are one of the best indicators of a city or village's allegiance with regard to the rebels' revolution.

In the last months of the Soviet Empire's decline, a first wave of *Leninopad*[12] swept across the land. Or rather, the land to the west, there where the Communist grafting never took. The former Polish Galicia swiftly got rid of its Lenins, the prime symbol of Soviet domination. Sometimes the past was recast at the same time. In Lviv, for example, the leader's bronze was melted down and recycled as a monument to the memory of the victims of Communist repression. Where you lived in Donetsk, as in Crimea, Lenin could sleep in peace. In central Ukraine, opinions were more divided, but inertia and indifference generally enabled them to stay put.

Until the Revolution of Dignity.

When things began to heat up on the Maidan, Lenin was put back on the agenda. As the Communist figure the most in view across the country, he became the symbol of Ukraine at the crossroads. To leave Vladimir Ilyich where he was, was to either wish for an alignment with Russia, or to resign oneself to the same thing. To bring him down meant, on the contrary, that one wanted Ukraine to take the European path.

One December night in 2013, ten days after the violence surrounding the fir tree, demonstrators with sledgehammers overturned the Lenin on Shevchenko Boulevard, right in the heart of the capital. The monument had

---

[12] "The fall of Lenin"

up to then survived all revolutions, shifts in power, political storms, and de-communization episodes.

This was the opening shot of a new *Leninopad*. Depending on the intensity of the violence on the Maidan, more or fewer statues fell each day. The record was set on February 22, 2014, the day when the revolution proclaimed its victory over Yanukovych. In 24 hours, 136 Lenins found themselves face to the ground.

Logically, it's central Ukraine that saw the greater number fall, before and after the revolution. The west had nothing more to demolish. In your city, Lenin was transformed, despite himself, into an icon of resistance against the "fascist junta."

And as long as the rebels remain in place, Lenin will be able to hold onto his streets, squares, and statues.

★★★

In front of the Sloviansk city hall, the anti-Lenins pass a rope around the disputed statue. The knot is tightened at its bronze feet. A dozen people grab hold of the rope and pull on it without really exerting themselves.

"Fall, Lenin!"

The gesture is symbolic. Just as symbolically, an old man leans against the pedestal, his arms spread out like a bodyguard trying to protect his superior from an angry crowd.

- No, but why are you doing this? You want to get rid

of Sloviansk's liberator? To replace him with Bandera?[13]

- No one's talking about Bandera here. We're doing this for justice.

- What justice? You haven't seen enough television to know what's going on here? Forget all this!

For now, Lenin will remain on his pedestal. But the past can bide its time.[14]

---

[13] Stepan Bandera, the controversial Ukrainian nationalist leader during the Second World War.

[14] Five months later, Sloviansk's municipal council will vote to keep the statue. Despite that, the following day at dawn, a nationalist group will bring it down.

Chapter 6

SASHA

A café-bar in Kramatorsk, about eight o'clock. A couple of tables away, two men and a woman are getting drunker by the minute, thanks to beer and vodka. I catch bits of their conversation. They're talking about the conflict and its consequences. Meanwhile, another woman goes to chew out a waiter at the bar. She accuses him of being impolite and deliberately turning his back on her when she calls to him. The three drinkers get themselves organized. They ask for the complaint book at the counter and pass it from table to table to have it signed by others. "Write about how great the service is here!" I'm talking on the telephone. I sign in order to get rid of the drunkards, and I go on with my call. They go back to their table. Their discussion becomes ever more feverish. They're not arguing. They're on the same wavelength. Suddenly, one of the men stands up and overturns the table. The empty glasses and plates crash to the ground. He points a finger at the only other clients in the room: a foreigner, seated at a table in front of mine, and me. Among the words coming out of his mouth, gone slack with alcohol, I only recognize "monkeys" and "pederasts." He's angry, but not threatening. He'd in any case be much too drunk to fight. They leave the premises. The woman pays, and apologizes to the waiters over and over again. After a few minutes, the man returns and excuses himself in turn. "It's the clients you should be apologizing to," replies a waiter. He does not, and leaves again. I ask the server what the man has against us. "I don't know. Maybe it's because you're foreigners. Political reasons. There's a conflict here, you know." The police arrive a bit later. The waiters tell them to let things drop. They leave. The man comes in again. He's with the woman. He apologizes once more. When he turns towards me, I politely invite him to sit at my table.

His name is Aleksander. Sasha.

"I was just wondering why you were angry with me."

He tries to talk to me in English and German, two languages that he obviously doesn't know, even when he's sober. Every once in a while, I repeat that I understand Russian. His narrative is disjointed, but by piecing together the fragments, I end up understanding his story.

It happened one September night, ninety kilometres south of the café-bar. A missile hit his apartment in Donetsk. He and his pregnant wife survived. Not their fifteen-year-old son. He pulls a passport out of his pocket. It's his son's. A stamp designates the day of his death: *September 12, 2014*. Their apartment was located near the Donetsk airport, where there was fierce fighting. The baby is now three weeks old. Who fired the shell? "The

Russians." He's certain of that, given its trajectory. "I had a car, a business, two apartments, and a son. I lost everything. What do I do now? I think of taking a revolver, and *pow*!" He mimes his suicide, a bullet in his head. After his son's death, he and his wife took refuge in Kramatorsk. "It's the asshole of the world here. There's nothing to do." He says he tried to join the Ukrainian army. "They don't want me because I'm from Donetsk." Since he only left some months after the start of the rebellion, he's considered to be a possible spy for the separatists. "Anyway, I couldn't bear seeing one of my friends in my gun sight. Half of them joined the rebels. The bastards." And he can no longer go back to Donetsk. "There, they'd take me for a *banderovets*," a Ukrainian nationalist. An enemy on one side, an enemy on the other. In his own country. Without having done anything to anyone. Without having any enemies himself.

From time to time, Sasha darts a look at the foreigner sitting behind us. He finds him suspicious. He tries to attract his attention, but he doesn't react, and keeps on drawing or writing in his notebook. I know him, in fact, this foreigner. We'd been introduced the day before, and had even shared a taxi with a friend we have in common. He's an American, and works for an international organization. When he came into the café, strangely, he didn't greet me, and since then he's ignored me, avoiding eye contact. I also find him shady, but I don't make anything of it. Sometimes I prefer naivety to paranoia. Whether he's an agent in disguise or a true member of the organization he claims to represent makes little difference. Sasha's not telling me any state secrets. "Is he one of yours?" I say no. It would be too complicated to explain to a drunk and suspicious man why two foreigners who know each other and find themselves in the same café are sitting at different tables and ignoring each other.

Sasha apologizes for his behaviour, and his current state. He asks me to understand why he drank so much this night. His son. Exile. A lost life. What's more, his mother lives in Crimea. Two weeks ago, the Ukrainian government permanently interrupted train and bus services in the direction of the peninsula, now under Russian control. "It's all shit. *Verstehen?* Understand?"

The café-bar is getting ready to close. It's barely 9:30. The woman who was drinking with Sasha joins us. It's his wife, Yulia. She apologizes in her turn and wishes me happiness and success, while trying to persuade her husband to follow her to the exit. The couple starts talking very loudly in Ukrainian. It's clearly not their mother tongue, nor the one they usually use between themselves. It's a profession of faith for the homeland of two people from Donetsk who left the rebel territory too late. Yulia ends the discussion with the rallying cry of the nationalists. "Glory to Ukraine! To the heroes, glory!"

We all head for the door.

Chapter 7

DONETSK

We're approaching the Kurakhove checkpoint. Before, it was a Donbas village among others. The war's vagaries have made it a frontier. It's here that my colleagues and I have to change cars and drivers. The Ukrainian authorities have just tightened the rules at crossing points. Soon - no one knows exactly when - the soldiers will demand one more piece of paper from whoever wants to enter or return from separatist territory. To obtain it, they'll have to wait in line in an administrative building - no one yet knows where - and prove that they have a good reason to go to Donetsk or to come back. Failing that, they'll have to pull out a large bank note to persuade the bureaucrat to hand over a pass despite everything. The rebels are those who split up the country, but it's the Ukrainian bureaucracy that's in charge of solidifying that division. Two months ago, the government stopped paying bureaucrats and retirees who remained in the self-proclaimed republics. It stopped financing schools, universities, hospitals, and other public services. The Ukraine National Bank ordered banks to close their branches in those zones, and to call a halt to all their financial transactions.

Every day that passes, you and your family are living less and less in Ukraine.

A businessman is negotiating with the soldiers at the checkpoint. He's from Donetsk. His car is full of merchandise. He assures them that his papers are in order, as was the case on previous days when he made the same trip. In vain. Today, he has to turn around and go back.

The soldiers aren't interested in our ATO press passes, though they were given to us by their superiors. The document has been valid for some days, but the orders have not yet reached Kurakhove. They want to see our passports.

The last checkpoint before no man's land. An electric pylon has come down in the nearby field. The cables are brushing against the frozen grain. The harvest will not be good this year. The post's sentry box is made up of a series of sandbags piled one on top of the other. Trenches have been dug in the surrounding fields. We are in 2015; you'd think it was 1915, during the Great War.

A few hundred metres of neutrality farther on, and we're in rebel territory. It only takes two or three minutes, but we're an hour later: the Donetsk People's Republic functions on Moscow time, and no longer that of Kyiv. In the distance we can see a coal mine. We pass a first separatist checkpoint, then a second. On a building in the first village, graffiti: *The sun loves the people. Hurrah!*

We come to Donetsk. You're more than a million people living there. A good many left the city at the height of the fighting, but a large number returned during the calm of the last months. Your family never left.

The rebel Donetsk is trying to erase its Ukrainian past. At certain traffic circles, Донецьк has become Донецк. The soft sign (ь), which sets the Ukrainian pronunciation slightly apart from the Russian, has been removed. Billboards are still talking about the separatist election of two months ago. Others exhort Donetsk citizens to enlist in the republic's army to "defend Donbas." All that's left of Ukraine are indecipherable shreds of paper on a few hoardings.

We go straight to the regional administration, situated in the building that the anti-Maidan demonstrators occupied several times before finally proclaiming their republic. In the entry hall, a photo of a plane. "People of the Popular Republic of Donetsk mourn the victims of Malaysian Airlines' Boeing 737, who died following the Ukrainian Army's war crime." The text is in English and Russian. All indications now point, however, to the rebels being responsible for the deaths of 298 people on board Flight MH17, shot down over the DPR on July 17, 2014. In the first hours, the rebel leaders even congratulated themselves on having brought down yet another Ukrainian military plane flying over their territory. When they realized their mistake, they got rid of all traces of the claim they'd made. Since then, the Russian media have come up with a series of alternative facts:

the Ukrainians mistook their target while trying to assassinate Vladimir Putin, whose airplane is white, red, and blue, like that of the Malaysian Airlines;

the CIA sent aloft a plane filled with dead bodies in order to explode it over rebel skies, so as then to cast blame on the militias.

With this propaganda, Tyoma, they were wagering that given all these versions, however absurd, the *actual* truth will be viewed as only one possibility among others. I'd like to tell you that the Ukrainian side is more honest, that it's able to recognize its failings in order to find itself worthy of its revolutionary ideals. But your own death will soon show that that is not the case.

★★★

More than a hundred people are standing in line in front of a building identified as a "Supermarket," near the Donetsk circus. Mainly elderly people and young mothers. The supermarket is one no longer. It's one of the distribution points of humanitarian aid for the Rinat Akhmetov Fund. The most powerful oligarch in the region, who has to placate both Kyiv and the separatists, indirectly buys his own peace by supplying rations to the old and vulnerable who no longer receive anything from the Ukrainian state, and not much more from the rebel government.

We are clearly not welcome. Very quickly, the fund's employees come to give us trouble. The DPR's press card, which we've just been granted, is of no use. They demand that we obtain special permission from the director of their organization.

- People are waiting, cold and hungry, and you've come to disturb them.

The ill-tempered beneficiaries join in.

- You want to show how much we're suffering, is that it?

- Write in French that everything is fine here, that our only problem is the Ukrainians who are bombing us!

- An old man even shouts: Get out the sticks and the sacks!

In the face of such hostility, we take our leave.

At the start of the rebellion in April, 2014, nostalgic grandmothers brandished portraits of Stalin in front of the Donetsk regional headquarters, demanding the return of the Soviet Union. Well, here it is: endless waiting lines for food, as in the worst years of the Communist regime. That said, the problem is not exactly the same as it was then. In the USSR, products were unavailable on the shelves because of natural or artificial shortages. Today, despite the growing bureaucratic difficulties for the transporters, Donetsk continues to receive shipments from the rest of Ukraine. It's not business as usual, but the merchants make do. What's lacking is the money to buy the products. For those in dire need, humanitarian aid partially helps to offset the difficulties in obtaining their pensions or some monetary support from one or other of the administrations.

The following day, we visit another distribution centre. This time a spokesperson for the Rinat Akhmetov Fund makes sure that no one will stop us from interviewing those receiving help. No special permission has ever been necessary. Uncertain, the Supermarket employees had just invented obstacles in order to protect themselves.

I begin the discussion with Yulia Nikolayevna, a woman in her sixties, or perhaps her seventies. She has a coupon in her hands and is waiting to receive a bag of groceries intended for retirees. In ten minutes, an hour, two or more, she will be given a kilo of rice, buckwheat, oil, canned food, matches, a few other essential products, and a box of chocolate to celebrate, belatedly, the New Year. But we talk less of this help than of the political reasons for her standing in line today.

"When did we become enemies of the Ukrainians? When there was a coup d'état in Kyiv. It was led by the Jews. Poroshenko is Jewish, Yatsenyuk is Jewish. Before that, we lived in harmony. Donbas is a multi-ethnic place. We don't understand Ukrainian very well, so Russian is our common language. We rose up so they wouldn't destroy our cities. It's the Americans who put Poroshenko in power. They wanted to get closer to the Russian border. What we want is to create a *Malorossiya*, a Little Russia. In the end, it doesn't matter if it's part of Ukraine or Russia. For now, we're still officially in Ukraine. Maybe it will all end with a federalization of the country. At present, you can't be categorically for or against any option. But what we really want is a flourishing country. A country where we're not being killed. A country that will not make us slaves. A country where we can work for what is good. And the only country that can give us that, I believe, is Russia."

I don't reply. The anti-Semitic paranoia is a belief. A belief implies a faith that is blind to its contradictions. Yulia *knows*, despite the facts. There is no way I can persuade her that neither the prime minister nor the president is Jewish. But what depresses me the most, without really surprising me, is that she imagines a radiant future for her self-proclaimed republic if it's annexed to Putin's Russia.

I'm going to confess something, Artyom. You've probably already noticed that I'm not trying to defend one camp or the other in this conflict. On the contrary, I'm trying to show that each one shares part of the blame for the dramatic sequence of events. The Maidan revolutionaries, the separatist rebels, Russia, but also the European Union and NATO. What concerns me is the effect their decisions and actions have had on innocents like yourself. My hope is that the war will end as quickly as possible, and that in its aftermath those who will have survived will have the right to peace and a better future. That is why Yulia's illusions sadden me. Russia, a thriving country where no one is killed, where the citizens are not slaves and where one works for the good? Really? After the five years during which I lived there, travelled and worked there, meeting Russians of all origins, social ranks, and political orientations, I would be inclined to paint a very different picture. For example, I remember a woman, Tatyana, living in a muddy village without gas or hot water, only 80 kilometres from a bustling Moscow. She described to me a Russia under Vladimir Putin that closely resembled that of Yulia. She only interrupted her rapturous discourse when I asked her whether, personally, she had seen any improvement in her life during Putin's supposedly golden age. "No, but you know, we're just little people." Her neighbour Raisa, just as dithyrambic where the president was concerned, admitted that she could not even allow herself to buy butter. Tatyana and Raisa's perception of their country had been forged by the daylong flow of propaganda on television, rather than by their own experience of what was real. On television, no one talked about the abuse of power, acts of violence, injustice and corruption, all attributable to the arbitrary nature of an authoritarian regime. What was bad was always an isolated incident or something that arrived from outside, it was never anything systemic.

I can of course understand Yulia Nikolayevna's reservations when it comes to Kyiv's nationalist government, which did not take the concerns of Russian speakers in the east seriously at a very critical juncture. I can also understand that she feels closer to Russia, culturally, socially, and historically.

True: in the short term, she would probably receive a more generous retirement pension if Donetsk were part of Russia rather than Ukraine.

True: her language would be better recognized and more respected, being the language of the majority.

True: Ukraine's progress towards Europe will be long and arduous, and Europe is no panacea. It has its own economic crises. Its state authorities sometimes kill their citizens. Working conditions are not always ideal, and private interests too often take precedence over the common good.

But my instinct tells me that, despite all these drawbacks, the European option is still the better one for all Ukrainians, even the Russian speakers in the east. In adopting it, they would have a better opportunity to achieve dignity, justice, equity, stability, and even material comfort, than if they opt for Russia's authoritarian model. Except that today, with the fears, the deaths, and the growing resentment, this assessment can only have a minimal influence on people's choices. Kyiv will have a hard time convincing Yulia Nikolayevna that she can one day, again, feel at home in Ukraine.

A certain Andrey joins the discussion. He's forty-four years old. He's come looking for a bag of groceries for his sick mother. "While they were demonstrating on the Maidan, we were continuing to work." It's a way of speaking: Andrey is unemployed. Still, his words reflect the widespread feelings of the Donbas worker, that the European dream is a whim of bourgeois nationalists. Here, prosperity is being built by digging in a mine or in forging metal, Andrey implies. Not in chasing rainbows.

When he went to vote "yes" in the separatist referendum of May 2014, Andrey did not dream that the situation would degenerate as it has. "We were voting for independence, but we thought that in the end we would have a federation, more autonomy for our region, or something like that. I thought that we would always be attached to Kyiv, but that they would let us live in our language and according to our traditions." He had certainly not anticipated a war. For him, blame for the escalation falls squarely on the shoulders of the Kyiv revolutionaries. "The first to take up arms were the people from the Maidan."

Andrey ends our conversation with a quotation from the former Russian prime minister, Viktor Chernomyrdin: *We wanted the best. And we got the same as usual.*

What must therein be understood: the corruption of ideals, and self-destruction.

Chapter 8

WHO KILLED ANATOLY IVANOVICH?

The first funeral I attended in Donbas was not yours, but that of Anatoly Ivanovich Karpov. He was 60 years old and he'd died as the result of a banking error. You can sift through the circumstances of his death for as long as you like, but in the end, without the banking error, he'd still be tending his vines and taking care of his grandchild in his Shakhtyorsk house.

Mister Karpov was a retired worker. But not someone who was retired from work. In theory he'd already taken his leave from the local coal enrichment factory. Except that his mechanic's pension was much too meagre to satisfy the needs of his household. And so he'd resigned himself to keep on working for as long as he still had the strength.

Two weeks before his death, he received a text message. A significant sum of money had been removed from his account in the Oschad Bank. Except he had made no such transaction. He called the bank, and he was told to resolve the problem at their nearest branch. Now, it had been a month since all the banks in Shakhtyorsk, as elsewhere in the separatist territories, had had to close their doors or be sanctioned by the Ukraine National Bank. Anatoly Ivanovich had to get himself to a branch on the Ukrainian side, and to do so, had to cross the front line.

The news of the suspect transaction came on December 29, the time of year when businesses, banks, and institutions all limit their activities. He decided to wait a few days before undertaking the trip.

Meanwhile, fighting broke out again.

He and his daughter Olga made their preparations. They would go together to Volnovakha. As Olga was an accountant, she could deal with figures, and knew how to handle the disagreement with the bank. They would take a bus, because to go in their car would be too costly. In this time of war, gas was more and more expensive.

In the early morning of January 13, 2015, they got on the bus. Four hours later, after having stopped in all the towns and villages along the way, and having passed both separatist and Ukrainian roadblocks, they arrived in Volnovakha. The branch of the Oschad Bank was situated on May 1st Street. They left with the assurance that the money would soon reappear in the account.

It was on the return trip that the war caught up with them. The bus was packed. Anatoly Ivanovich had a seat. Olga was standing in the aisle. A young man offered her his seat. She politely declined the offer. At the last Ukrainian roadblock, on the way out of Volnovakha, the soldiers stopped the bus on the side of the road to check the passengers' papers. The passengers had been waiting for ten minutes when a rocket fell beside the road, fifteen metres from the bus. All the windows were blown out. Ten of the passengers died on the spot, including the polite young man who had offered his seat to Olga. Anatoly Ivanovich arrived at the Volnovakha hospital in critical condition. After a four-hour operation he breathed his last, becoming the explosion's eleventh victim. A little later it was the turn of a 24-year-old young woman, and the day after, that of an old man, bringing the toll to 13 victims.

As Olga is telling me her story, she's still under observation in the hospital. Shrapnel is lodged in her left shoulder and arm. "If I'd sat down when the boy offered me his place, I'd be dead. It's hard to live with the idea that one moment you're beside a loved one, and the next, he's not there." The reasons other survivors were on the bus are as banal as that of the Karpovs:

> Valery was returning from a visit to his sister on the Ukrainian side;
> Vladimir went to pick up the birth allowance for his daughter-in-law's baby;
> others were coming back with their old age pension money.

The restrictions imposed on the separatist territories by the Ukrainian government had complicated everyone's life. They still considered themselves Ukrainian citizens, but had the misfortune of living in the wrong place. Getting around the restrictions to lay their hands on what was owed them had become a risky venture.

★★★

Anatoly Ivanovich's funeral took place at his home in Shakhtyorsk, three days after his death. Olga succeeded, after much effort, in repatriating her father's body.

The Karpov house is easy to find, on The Internationale Street. There are several cars parked in front. Fifteen or so relatives and friends have already arrived. My colleagues and myself find Anatoly Ivanovich in the living room, laid out in his coffin. His widow and his old mother are weeping by his side. Between sobs, they pronounce a few words aloud, presumably for our benefit.

- He worked all his life! Forty, fifty years!
- He helped all those who needed it!
- We were always together, in work and on vacation.
- *They* will keep on until there are none of us left. I want peace now, nothing else!
- We're all the same, why are we killing each other?

Their political allusions are vague. They do not say who, according to them, is responsible for the death of their loved one. The Karpov family does not want any trouble. Interviewed on camera, Olga remains cautious.

- Talk to us about your father.
- He was a good man. If not, there wouldn't be so many people at his funeral.
- What happened exactly?

- I don't really remember the explosion…

As soon as the journalist puts down the camera, she speaks more freely.

- Of course the firing came from the rebel positions.

Her version agrees with that of the Ukrainian army: the separatists were aiming at the military roadblock, and they were a bit off target. The bus passengers are collateral damage, but in the opinion of the Ukrainian authorities, that proves that the rebels don't care about civilians. Since the event, they've been flaunting the example of this attack in all the international forums. As for the rebels, they claim that the shell could not have been launched from their territory. They insist that their closest position is fifty kilometres from the Ukrainian roadblock, and that it does not have weapons powerful enough to strike so far away. Given this premise, they propose different theories, including that of a mine that the Ukrainians themselves planted near the bus, then activated in order to be able to accuse the separatists of the death of innocent civilians.

Who, then, killed Anatoly Ivanovich and the twelve other passengers on the bus from Volnovakha?

Logic and a few clues point to the rebels. But guilt in wartime is a question not of facts, but of opinion.

"Do your really think that *our people* could have killed their own like that? It's a provocation, nothing else. The Ukrainians orchestrated everything."

These words are being uttered in the Karpov house's entry hall, barely a few metres from Anatoly Ivanovich's corpse. The speaker is a niece of the dead man, also called

Olga. She has come with her mother from Snezhnoye, another mining town not far off.

Same family, a different version.

★★★

After the burial, the Karpovs invite us to the Rendezvous Café for a gathering in honour of the deceased. A former colleague of Anatoly Ivanovich speaks: "We began working together at the factory at the same time. He was always a good worker. He was kind. Let's not talk about politics today. Let's remember how he was a good man."

In private, however, Olga confessed to me that her father detested the rebels who controlled her city. "He complained about them a lot. He'd been part of the factory's management, and he knew perfectly well that heavy industry in Donbas only functioned thanks to subsidies that came from Kyiv. He was certain that it wasn't a good idea to separate."

During the meal, Anatoly Ivanovich's widow talked to us about her husband's gifts as a wine grower. "He published his own little paper on wine growing. We always waited at least five years before opening up a vintage. What you're drinking now dates from 2008. There's no water in this wine. I had a good husband."

I can't tell you why exactly, Tyoma, but that's what touched me the most at Anatoly Ivanovich's funeral. He'd not foreseen his death, and yet he had something to offer us from beyond the grave to honour his memory: a sweet wine that he'd produced himself from the grapes in his garden.

Saying goodbye, Sasha, Karpov's son, invited me to visit again the following September, during the harvest: "I may marry then, and for the occasion we'll open a bottle from 1979, the year of my birth."

In the end, Anatoly Ivanovich had anticipated everything. Life will go on without him, but he'll still play a small part in it.

Chapter 9

A PILE OF RUINS

Waiting for Aleksander Zakharchenko to arrive - he's late - I reread on my telephone his biographical details. He was born, grew up, studied, and worked in Donetsk. He began his career as an electrician in a mine, but he didn't stay there very long. Like most resourceful and ambitious individuals in these post-Soviet territories, he soon launched himself into business, the kind with one foot in legality, and the other on the fringes of the official economy. He also for a long time preferred to practise politics on the margins of the system. He directed the local branch of Oplot ("Rampart"), an organization that helped out families of policemen killed on the job, and veteran soldiers, while opposing the elevation to heroic stature of Ukrainian nationalists who had collaborated with the Nazis. In addition, Oplot was a mixed martial arts club. At the beginning of the counter-revolution in Donbas, the organization became an armed battalion, and Zakharchenko, a warlord. And here he is now, less than a year later, at the age of 38, prime minister of the self-proclaimed Donetsk Popular Republic, coming into a conference room in battledress, a pistol on his belt, flanked by his personal guard.

"Dear journalists, I don't have much time. I have to get to the airport with the OSCE.[15] Please limit yourselves to one question." He has no flight to catch at the Sergey Prokofiev airport. Planes haven't been flying for several months. What awaits him are the fierce combats that are raging, and that seem to be reaching their end point. Ukrainian soldiers are again dug in at the airport's new terminal. For weeks they've been resisting rebel attacks. In the Ukrainian imagination, these are the "cyborgs", half-man and half-machine, supreme resistance heroes facing up to the "terrorists" who are tearing the country apart.

For Zakharchenko and his men, a victory would be more symbolic than strategic. The airport, completely renovated barely three years ago, is now but a pile of ruins. The day before yesterday, even the control tower crumbled. It would take months and hundreds of millions of dollars - which the DPR does not have - to make it functional again.

Yes, you've understood right, Artyom. The echoes of fighting that you hear all the way to your house a few days from your death, are men killing and dying for the control of valueless ruins. They are fighting so that their leader can in the end puff out his chest for a few seconds before thinking about his next conquest.

---

[15] Organization for Security and Co-operation in Europe

"At this very moment, we are finishing up the 'cleansing' of the airport. About ninety-five per cent of the new terminal is already ours. But there is still some resistance. The Ukrainian soldiers do not want to surrender. Except that unfortunately for them, the "cyborgs" are not up to functioning well in our wintry conditions. I think that, in thirty or so minutes, the airport will be entirely under our control."

For Zakharchenko, the Ukrainian powers alone are to be blamed for the recent renewal of hostilities and for their prolongation.

"We are ready for any discussion. We do not want this war. It's not easy at this point in time. The Minsk[16] accords have been broken. There is heavy combat. Our brothers and sisters are dying. Respected journalists, I am officially inviting Petro Poroshenko to the Donetsk airport. He is the commander in chief of the Ukrainian forces. He is the president of Ukraine. As leader, he has an obligation to think of his citizens. If he's a man, if he's not afraid of being president, let him stop the fighting and come. I guarantee his safety, one hundred per cent. We're going to sit at the negotiating table right there in the new airport terminal. We'll drink tea and talk. He can see what he has done."

At that moment, I can see how Aleksander Zakharchenko, with his roly-poly, sympathetic baby face, hard and authoritarian, however, like that of a soldier, has been

---

[16] The first peace agreement signed on September 5, 2014, violated immediately.

able to scale the ladder of the rebel hierarchy right to the top. His rhetoric is populist. He knows how to advocate the impossible in order afterwards to accuse the other side of failure. His deceitful intentions are in no way troubled by the truth.

"Ukraine sees our kindness as a weakness. We are not weak. We are just people who don't want to resolve important questions with arms. We've already shown that we are capable of taking the airport if we so choose. We have not done so before today because we thought that the Ukrainians would themselves understand and would surrender. From a strategic point of view, this airport is nothing. But the battle has enabled us to demonstrate that Ukraine is not up to undertaking any kind of military operation with success. They are not soldiers. If they do not know how to fight, what are they doing here? Let them stay home and take care of their children, of their state. It's better for them not to show up here. No one has ever succeeded in bringing Donbas to its knees. It's not Ukraine that's going to do it. Attacking a bus full of civilians in Volnovakha, firing on a hospital while there's a woman giving birth inside, only Ukraine can do that. Electricity is not cut off when the Ukrainians bombard us. Our houses are well heated. Food is less expensive than in Ukraine. Now gas is also cheaper. Petro Poroshenko can come and see for himself. He'll be warmly welcomed. His soldiers will finally get new clothes and hot tea. Our current problem is sabotage on the part of the Ukrainians. We've already begun to provide welfare to our population, but it's not happening as quickly as we would like. We must fight, and at the same time, restart our economy. Freedom is expensive."

After having said everything and its opposite, Zakharchenko rises. It's time to leave for the airport. My colleagues and I pile into our car, and follow his convoy. No decision has actually been taken. It's the logical outcome of our coverage of the day's events. So it is that at one moment in your life, after having sworn not to do such a thing, you find yourself in peril, driving towards an airport being bombarded from every side, wondering if it's safer to fasten your seatbelt in case of an accident, or not to do so in order to get out of the vehicle more easily in case of an explosion, and if it's better to pull on a bulletproof vest to protect yourself from shrapnel, or not to do so in order to run faster in case of shooting nearby.

★★★

We stop in the middle of a frozen dirt road. The neighbourhood of wooden houses nearby has suffered greatly from the fighting during recent months. The inhabitants have fled. All that's left are a few dogs, loose or tied up, to keep guard over the devastation. I've never heard bombardments so close by since my arrival in Donetsk. I've never heard bombardments so close by in my entire life. We're barely a kilometre from the airport. Zakharchenko is there. He's swapped his pistol for a machine gun. He's talking to a soldier from the Vostok battalion, who is leading the offensive on the new terminal. A group of journalists, mainly Russian, is gathered round him. Besides the rebel militiamen, other soldiers are present. Two have a Ukrainian flag sewn onto their uniforms, three have one that's Russian. They're all part of a group coordinating a ceasefire, supervised by the OSCE. Officially, the Russian officers are not participating in the conflict, but are just mediators. But everyone knows that their country is arming the rebels, advising them, and providing them with men. Together, these men are supposed to be *building the peace* while their fellows are dropping bombs on heads right nearby.

Zakharchenko approaches the microphones and cameras. "This is our land here. My children were born here and grew up here. My grandfathers and great grandfathers are buried here. All these homes destroyed…" An explosion very close by interrupts him. The journalists shudder. He carries on with the assurance of someone who's seen it all. "Don't be afraid, it's not that close. When you hear a shell whistling, you still have four seconds and a half to take cover."

On the periphery, a Ukrainian officer is voicing his opinion on the fighting to other journalists. He's at least a head taller and a decade older than Zakharchenko. "We can't stop defending ourselves. Our soldiers are dying in the terminal. When they stop attacking, we'll stop shooting. But there's no question of our abandoning our land."

- Hey, look over there!

Zakharchenko comes within a few centimetres of the

Ukrainian. They're now face to face, and he pokes his rebel index finger into the other's chest, while taking him to task.

- That's my aunt's house. Do you mean to tell me that this is what they're dying for, your soldiers, your monsters, your good-for-nothings? I'm saying this right to your face: I'm going to crush anyone who comes here with a weapon, dammit! This is *my* land!

- My father's house is on Petrovka Street and it's been destroyed!

- It's your soldiers who did that. Understand? They're the ones who destroyed it!

A soldier orders the journalists to disperse: "Turn off your cameras! Clear out!" The Ukrainian officer goes silent. He'll talk to no one any more. His comrade, Colonel Petro Kanonik, is more forthcoming. "Ah! You're from Canada. So you're on our side." I make it clear that I do not represent my government, and that I am not taking sides in this conflict. I say it very loudly, so that the journalists for the Russian propaganda networks don't get the bright idea, in their reporting, of saying I'm in collusion with the Ukrainians. My warning in no way lessens the colonel's desire to confide in a Canadian.

"We were supposed to lead you to the airport some time ago, but Zakharchenko doesn't want to show you the new terminal until it's entirely in his hands. He's doing that for his image. Today, Russian and local television have broadcast reports saying that the airport belongs to the rebels. The truth is that it's the old terminal that's under their control, and the new one is ours. All they do is lie. You don't build a state with lies. I'm in touch with our men in the terminal. They're under heavy fire. But they're there to stay."

A little nearer to the airport, on Stratonauts Street, Colonel Kanonik spots a half-open garage. The ground in front of it is strewn with cartridge cases. Boxes of munitions are piled up just beside them. Opening the door, he discovers an armoured vehicle marked with two red stars, painted white to camouflage it in winter. He photographs it with his phone. The rebels don't stop him. They're not really watching him. A few steps from there, soldiers stand guard to stop the journalists from going any farther. Only two are authorized to accompany a separatist commando in the direction of the airport. Not surprisingly, the reporters chosen are from Russian television. A guard in the middle of the road is asked if he's afraid. He's calmly smoking a cigarette. He's not yet twenty years old. "Of course I'm afraid." His blank face, almost indifferent, hides the feeling contained in his words.

Zakharchenko starts talking again. "Yes, I lost my cool back there. But you know, it's very hard to see the destruction in these streets where I walked when I was a child. I don't understand why the Kyiv government decided to attack with tanks, artillery, and planes, a people that held a referendum to decide on its fate. On the Maidan, all sorts of slogans talked about equality, fraternity, and the fight against corruption. But in fact, we're the ones putting those ideals into practice, here.

"Donbas is a land of workers, miners, steel workers, farmers, fishermen, doctors, professors. While they were demonstrating on the Maidan, we kept on digging out coal, sowing wheat, catching fish, smelting metal. We know how to fight. Our grandfathers and great grandfathers fought against the fascists. We can't betray the blood in our veins. We can't forget the horrors the fascists committed. In Kyiv nowadays, they're organizing torchlight parades. Doesn't that remind you of something? Munich, 1937.[17] Haven't you noticed the resemblance? The swastikas, the torches. Soon they'll be burning books. And then what? Concentration camps? We're peaceful people. We want peace. Let God allow our children to live in peace and not to have to fight."

In the evening, The Russian television reports announce that the airport is wholly under rebel control, as Zakharchenko predicted. It's false. The fighting over the pile of ruins continues.

If it had come to an end on this day, you might still be alive.

---

[17] The most significant Nazi torchlight parade took place, rather, in Berlin in 1933, during Hitler's assumption of power.

Chapter 10

YOUR DEATH

It's Saturday afternoon, the day before your death, on Pushkin Boulevard in the centre of Donetsk. A man disguised as a penguin is distributing leaflets and apples to promote a dental clinic. "Come visit us!" he shouts to me through his thick costume.

In front of the DPR headquarters, a few dozen babushkas are voicing their unhappiness with the rebel authorities. They have fled the same streets near the airport where I followed Zakharchenko.

- I have to rent an apartment in town for a thousand hryvnias, but my pension is only nine hundred hryvnias a month!

- There are many empty apartments in Donetsk. They should give them to people like us who have no roofs over our heads!

A militiaman posted in front of the building finds me suspicious. He takes me by the arm and leads me aside to check my papers. Everything is in order. He lets me go.

In this midwinter, dangers are rife in the rebel capital. But much more than the bombs, the most serious threat to the ordinary pedestrian is right under his feet. The successive freezes and thaws have turned the sidewalks into a veritable skating rink. The municipal employees can scatter sand all they want to improve the traction, Donetsk is still extremely slippery. Walking demands a vigilance as concentrated as does listening for the artillery firings to determine where they're coming from and where they're going to land.

Another immediate danger: car accidents. The more intense the bombardments, the less drivers respect the rules of the road. In order to reduce the likelihood of receiving a missile on one's hood, they drive as fast as possible from point A to point B. Traffic lights and stop signs have become optional. Our driver Valera lost his son-in-law that way, going through a red light. The war had nothing to do with it. Or so little.

On arriving in Donetsk, I soon got used to distant bombs providing the background noise for everyday life. Every time the firing comes close on the other hand, I become uneasy.

In the sky these days, the birds in flight are jumpy and erratic. They don't like what they see, either.

In the evening, I get together with colleagues in the old apartment they've rented in the centre of town. The place has clearly not been renovated for at least three or four decades. In the living room there's an old combination record player and radio. A VEF model, out of a Riga factory, from a time when Latvia was part of the Soviet Union. The names of the Eastern Bloc cities are inscribed next to the frequencies. It was a time when the airwaves broadcast a single ideology. I plug in the machine and put a vinyl record on the turntable. It works. Or almost. There's a defective gear. Only one LP turns at the right speed. For the others, I have to rotate the disc with my finger, seeking the right rhythm, in the process creating psychedelic variants of the melodies. Truly, the world is not spinning as it should.

We drink, we laugh, we dance. The bombardments outside the window force us to live as best we can. To live, just in case.

Coming back to my hotel room a few streets away from the apartment, I happen on a surprise roadblock of militiamen. It's almost midnight, the curfew has been in force since eleven o'clock. They check my papers and tell me to get back to my hotel as fast as possible. At the Ekonom, the receptionist sighs with relief. She was worried that she hadn't seen me before the curfew came into effect. She'd tried to reach me, but my phone was off. She'd inquired about me with my journalist colleagues in the same hotel. Her concern was genuine, maternal. And, you know Tyoma, that reassured me. It reassured me to know that with all the despicable things going on around us, this lady could be anxious for me, an unknown, a foreigner. For a moment I felt less alone, and felt loved just for belonging to the human race.

FOR WANT OF A FIR TREE

★★★

The next day, I get up early. At least an hour before you die. The rockets have been raining down for a good part of the night, and it's still going on. Outside, the noise of the detonations mingles with the birdsong. The sun has not yet risen. Around ten past eight, just as the Grad rocket strikes your house and puts an end to what might have been your life, I'm getting ready for my day. On the news sites, I read that the Ukrainian forces have launched a major offensive aimed largely at retaking control of the Donetsk airport. This explains that. But what's preoccupying me the most is to find some Donbas businessmen who will agree to talk to me. I've promised an article to *La Presse* that would explain how they are able to run their businesses in a separatist republic cut off from the banking system and subject to many restrictions. For days I've been looking for someone to interview, but all those I've approached are suspicious. They don't want any problems with the Ukrainian authorities or with the rebels.

At about the time your life is coming to an end, I'm recording the bombardments on my phone. There is not yet any link in my head between these explosions and your fate. I may have recorded your death during those few seconds.

This morning, in several Ukraine cities, and even in front of the Russian embassies of Western capitals, thousands of people are demonstrating against the barbarism of the Donbas "terrorists" and their masters in Moscow.

The death of Anatoly Ivanovich and the twelve other passengers on the Volnovakha bus has affected them. Addressing the crowd in Kyiv, President Poroshenko vows that he has no intention of ceding "a single inch" of Ukrainian territory to the separatists.

Meanwhile, you're lying lifeless beneath the ruins of your house.

I get a call from the newspaper *La Croix*. They want a piece for the next day. I make my way to a children's hospital, shut down since the beginning of hostilities. A shell arrived a few hours ago and damaged the front of the building. In the shadows of an adjacent street, positioned discreetly, there is a rebel artillery piece mounted on a truck. It was probably the target of that shot.

In my article, I talk about you without even knowing it:

> Donetsk awoke under bombs and the odour of gunpowder yesterday, as the fighting intensified between the Ukrainian and rebel forces, over the control of the airport and nearby neighbourhoods. The city centre of the separatist capital, relatively spared for some weeks, was also hit. [...]
>
> Over recent days, the Ukrainians have come to recognize the gravity of the situation for the few soldiers still defending this symbolic stronghold, already in ruins for some time. It's to save these men, more and more isolated, according to the Ukrainian Army's Anti-terrorist Operation, that the army has launched an attack in the early morn-

ing, claiming that it wants to *"choke off the artillery positions of the enemy that is firing"* on the airport. [...]

The Kyiv army declared that it lost four soldiers during the operation, which has extended to other zones on the front line. Thirty-two other soldiers have been wounded. The municipal authorities of Donetsk, under rebel control, have announced that two civilians lost their lives during the bombardments.

At this point, for me, you're just one half of the number two.

Chapter 11

EPIPHANY

It's Epiphany today, and you're lying in the morgue, between death and burial. The sky is calmer than yesterday. I go with some of my colleagues to a restaurant not far from what's left of your house. There's a large wooden terrace next to a pond with a dock extending into it. At its end, two stairways have been installed so that the faithful may step down into the water, partly freed from ice for the occasion. It's here that they will go, as they do every year, to submerge themselves three times, in the name of the Father, the Son, and the Holy Ghost. Loudspeakers are already belching out Russian pop music. The first brave souls jump into the water. A group of soldiers arrives. Among them is Denis, thickset, "31 years old, almost 32." His features are drawn and haggard. He and his comrades have arrived from the front. Their commander has given them a three-hour leave for the celebration. Denis has come to immerse himself, to "protect his body and mind from the war." Still, he assures us that he's not afraid while he's fighting the enemy. "Truth is on our side." Just a year ago, Denis was working on construction sites in a united Ukraine. He became a soldier "because of the Maidan." He will stop being one "when the Kyiv junta will leave Donbas alone." I ask him where he sees himself on the same date next year. "I'll be a victor in the war, and I'll take part in a parade through the city."

A priest appears. He positions himself, lights candles, and begins a mass, facing believers in bathing suits, underclothes, and dressing gowns. Denis prays along with the others. The priest blesses them. Armoured trucks pass along the road bordering the pond. The crowd watches them. Some take photos. Once the mass is finished, everyone gets in line to plunge into the water. A blonde little girl approaches with her mother. She's the age you still were yesterday, perhaps younger. She hesitates to jump. Her mother insists a little, picks her up, and brings her feet close to the icy surface. "I don't want to!" repeats the girl, whining. Her mother puts her back on solid ground.

Would you have jumped in if you were still alive?

★★★

I talk with a Cossack. He's wearing a tall grey astrakhan hat, and a navy blue uniform. He's in his late sixties, and has a well-trimmed white beard. Konstantin Chudakov has been told that he's too old to fight. He helps the rebellion out as best he can. "We're fighting for our beliefs, for truth and justice, while the others are fighting for someone else." He means Americans or Europeans, probably both. For him, the "coup d'état" in Kyiv was a plan orchestrated by foreign powers to take control of Ukraine and remove it from the Russian orbit. "We lived well before. We respected one another. Then fascism arrived. After that, there was no more tolerance. Ukraine forbade us from speaking our language. We proposed a federation. We were not even thinking of leaving Ukraine at that time. But they didn't like that. Why? Because the rest of the country profits from the money being transferred from Donbas. And after that, we're the bad ones? Now we have to fight for our independence."

The Cossacks support the rebellion against Kyiv. Some regiments have even set up their own administration in certain locales, at times in competition with the central powers of the separatist republics. They claim to be continuing the struggle of the seventeenth and eighteenth century Cossack warriors, defenders of the unbreakable bond between Russia and Ukraine.

Curiously, the Ukrainian nationalists also lay claim to a Cossack heritage. To resist the police forces during the Euromaidan, they formed companies in line with the ancestral, centuria model, and proudly sang this passage from the Ukrainian national anthem:

Our soul and body, yea, our all,
offer we at freedom's call,

We, whose forebears and ourselves,
proud Cossacks are!

The nationalists' perception of this legacy could not be more different from that of the rebels: for them, these heroic ancestors are the precursors of a democratic Ukrainian state independent from Russia.

Same history, different reading.

What neither camp mentions, however, is that, to conquer their enemies, the historical Cossacks murdered, pillaged, and raped. They especially liked organizing pogroms against Jews. That is how their passion for liberty and justice was expressed. The Cossacks were no more bloodthirsty than other groups at a time when innocent heads rolled for trifles. But they were bloodthirsty all the same. How could the Maidan demonstrators claim to defend peace, freedom, and a respect for human rights, while harking back to those barbarian hordes? Will history not one day hand down to us enough heroes with clean hands, so that we won't have to fall back on yesteryear's butchers and destroyers to shore up our ideals? With models like that, it's no wonder that quarrels turn into bombings.

Chapter 12

YOUR FUNERAL

It's a vulture who led me to you.

"It seems that one of Sunday's victims was a four-year-old child."

Every morning on waking, the vulture hopes for others' deaths. He hopes for an explosion, bodies strewing the ground, and especially, to be able to arrive first at the scene of the drama to photograph it all. Otherwise, death would only be a waste of lives. That's what might be called a professional warp. Or rather, a warping of the profession. The vulture does not pay heed to what is real, he fantasizes about what he'd like to be. And yet we practise the same profession. As with him, tragedies earn me money.

Yes, your death is a good story. It will attract more attention than that of a soldier or a grandfather. I'll go to your funeral, I'll write your story. I won't mourn you. You're not my drama. You're only an innocent victim among others in this war; one among hundreds on the same day across the earth.

The only difference between the vulture and myself,

when you come down to it, is that I'll never be able to bring myself to relish the excellent story you've given us, before I move on to another.

★★★

The Donetsk morgue. A few months ago, a shell struck the building next door. The corpses almost died a second time. Inside, the putrefaction penetrates your nostrils at once. It clings to your clothes and your skin. Visitors cover their faces with handkerchiefs. The workers are used to it. You're lucky only in this: death spares you the odour of death.

In the ground floor corridor, an arm hangs from a stretcher. The rest of the body is properly covered. At the next stretcher, it's the toes that protrude from the sheet. The morgue is full to bursting. In the main mortuary room, lifeless humans are scattered pell-mell over the floor, in the corners, on tables, some in bags, others not. There's no refrigeration system.

We don't find you.

Second floor. The director's office. His name is Dmitri Kalashnikov. He has nothing to do with machine guns, but he often deals with those who have been gored by their shells. He asks us to sit down. "The current situation is like that of last summer, at the height of the fighting. We work seven days out of seven. We can't stop." The new year is only twenty days old, and the locations he oversees in the Donetsk region have already received

116 dead bodies. "They're for the most part victims of the war, and about three-quarters of them are civilians."

The vulture asks about you. Kalashnikov confirms that you died on Sunday, at 5 Ilinskaya Street. He gives us your father's phone number. We call him. He's in the hospital, at the bedside of your mother and your brother. She's just had her right leg amputated; your brother is fighting for the survival of his left eye. His family is in shreds, yet your father, despite everything, will make himself available to us. "Do you want me to come right away?" He has not seen your body since he found it in the ruins of your house two days ago. We head outside, behind the morgue, where the air is breathable.

A dozen people are standing about in the cold. It's here that the empty coffins are brought in before re-appearing with the remains. Some militiamen are getting ready to receive the bodies of two of their comrades. Those soldiers came from afar to die here. From Russia. They'd joined the Vostok rebel battalion and were killed on Sunday, like you, in the fighting for control of the airport.

The woman who provides us with these details goes by her nom de guerre: *Glaza*. "Eyes." Her nickname is inspired most certainly by her striking, green irises, the first thing you notice when you look at her. Like almost all the regular rebels, she does not reveal her true identity. One day, the war may end. And if Donbas becomes part of Ukraine once more, she will have to learn again to live with that fact, and to bury her separatist past. Glaza is 27 years old. She's become an ambulance driver at the front, even if she has no training, neither medical nor military. So it goes in wartime. She's the mother of an eight-year-old girl. During Euromaidan she was living in Kyiv, and was working for a clothing company. Some of her girlfriends went regularly to demonstrate on the square. Not her. After the revolution, she returned to Donbas to join the rebellion. She bought an apartment in Makeyevka, a Donetsk suburb. At least that's what she says. It's possible that she received it for services rendered to *Novrossiya*. Since she left Kyiv, her revolutionary friends have defriended her on social media. She's created new accounts. In Ukraine, she no longer exists. Here, her work consists in driving to the airport and bringing back the wounded and the dead. She often goes right into the thick of the fighting. Sometimes she gathers up enemy soldiers, dead or wounded, and takes them to a Ukrainian roadblock. Every time, she doesn't know if she'll be arrested by the government forces. She says she knows of only one instance where a wounded separatist was taken to a rebel roadblock by the Ukrainians. To her mind, virtue and honour exist on only one side of the front line.

Glaza has no time to explain why she chose to opt for the Donetsk Popular Republic to ensure a brighter future for her daughter. Her comrades' bodies are on their way out of the morgue in maroon coffins. They're placed in a truck and put on the road to Russia.

★★★

Your father Vladimir arrives. He seems more exhausted than grief stricken. He probably does not yet realize what has happened to you. Or perhaps he's forgotten it for a few seconds. He starts telling me about his Sunday.

It was ten past eight. He was on his way back from his night shift at the foundry. The rockets began to fall on the neighbourhood just as he was getting out of the minibus. He ran towards the house. When he arrived, your mother was trapped in the ruins and screaming. Your brother Misha was still conscious, but a piece of shrapnel was lodged in the middle of his forehead. His nose hung down. Your great grandmother was caught in the latrines in the back yard. She had survived a world war. She would be spared again, with just a minor wound in her leg. You, you were hidden beneath the ruins of the living room. You had already stopped breathing. "He'd just woken up. He was drinking tea. If he'd been in another room, he'd have been all right."

Your father has been wearing the same clothes since Sunday. His pants are torn. "I carried all my family out of the ruins with these hands. They were full of blood." He gropes in his coat pocket and brings out a carton of apple juice and a sweet. "He was waiting for me to give him this." It's at that moment that he starts to cry. Over the next hours, I'll see him shift from apathy to confusion to anger.

Your father is 30 years old. Today he seems ten or fifteen years older. The foundry that employs him is in rebel territory, but is still controlled by Ukrainian interests. All its production is sent to Ukraine. "That's where I pay my taxes. In other words, I myself have contributed to my family's murder. I don't understand this war. I was against it from the beginning. I'm not a soldier, I'm a worker. My father and grandfather were miners. We've always worked. We've never waited for anything to fall from the sky."

The double meaning of this metaphor is accidental.

"Who will give me back my son, now? Who will take responsibility for this attack? Who can I turn to so that the guilty will be punished? Who will want my family now, with its two disabled people? I don't understand how they can be proud of what they're doing, these prime ministers, these presidents. Why don't they want just to *live*, like me? And I don't understand the international community. They look away while criminals fire on civilian populations. Your governments are helping them to bomb us." He brings out his phone and shows me a photo of your brother and you taken on New Year's Day. That was three weeks ago. You're dressed up as a penguin. You smile.

"Do they look like terrorists?"

Your father is certain he knows where the shots came from: from Pesky, the last village under Ukrainian control before the rebel zone. That's where Ukrainian artillery is positioned. It's from there that it fires, mainly in the direction of the airport. "There was no military target within a kilometre of our house. They deliberately aimed at our neighbourhood."

His colleagues from the foundry arrive with flowers. They've helped organize the funeral, which will take place in less than an hour. They surround your father and talk to him. But suddenly, his face goes blank. He loses consciousness. His two feet start to slide. No one has time to catch hold of him. He falls like a dead weight onto the ice. His friends start to throw snow on his face, and to slap him. I give them my water bottle to splash him and have him drink. He wakes up as abruptly as he fainted, sucking in a huge gulp of air as if he were emerging from a bad dream, and coming back to the world. Except that his nightmare is in that world. His reprieve will have been brief. We bring him to his feet. His friends hold him by the shoulders. He grips my wrist tightly, and murmurs.

"The bastards, the bastards…"

The truck from the funeral service arrives. They've brought you a blue coffin. I wonder whether your father chose that colour. I wonder if he had to give them your measurements, or whether they've been estimated according to your age. The pallbearers go into the morgue to collect your body. They come out again after a few minutes. The coffin is open, but I can barely see you. You take up little space and they are holding you high. Your father and his friends form a small procession to accompany you to the truck. "Curse you, Poroshenko!" a woman exclaims. "The sons of bitches, the sons of bitches!" cries your father.

From a distance, we follow your procession to the cemetery. You will not be exposed in your house's living room as is the custom, and as it was for Anatoly Ivanovich the week before in Shakhtyorsk. You have no more house in which to be exposed.

A thick fog hovers over the Flora cemetery. When we arrive, your coffin has already been set on two stools beside the main road. Fifteen or so people are gathered in a semi-circle around you. There's Father Mikhail, your grandmother, a few close friends, your father, and his comrades from the foundry. On the other side there are us, eight journalists and photographers. Most of us try to be discreet. "Put something on his head!" demands your father. A prayer band is placed on your brow. Your grandmother sets your plush rabbit down by your side. She's inconsolable.

It's the first time that I can get a good look at you. Your skull seems to have been resewn. Your left cheek has been lacerated, either by shrapnel or by debris from the walls that fell on you.

The ceremony is far from peaceful. We soon realize that rebel artillery is positioned somewhere nearby, perhaps even in the cemetery. Since I've been in Donetsk, I've learned to tell the difference between shells coming in and shells going out. An off-target counterattack by the Ukrainians could fall on our heads at any moment. I look at you often, but never for too long. Each time, I shake my head slightly and take a step backwards. All this is surreal. It's the first time I've attended a funeral for a four-year-old child. It's the first time I've attended a funeral, while fearing for my life.

Two trucks loaded with a system of multiple Grad rocket launchers surge into view out of the fog. The forty cannons on each truck are empty. The gunners must have fired them off before our arrival. They pass by barely a metre from your loved ones. I take a picture of what caused your death thumbing its nose at what it has wrought. Every reason to despise hate, to oppose war, is there in a single frame:

> you, dead;
> your dear ones, distraught;
> and those machines, intact, which, with the same criminal negligence, have killed and will kill more Artyoms, Darias, Marias, or Aleksys along one stretch or another of the front line, machines that decimate generations while claiming to defend the future.

I look at you in your coffin, and I imagine those leaders, enemies today, who will find themselves tomorrow or some time later in the palatial hall of a neutral capital, signing a peace agreement. They will shake hands for a long time, smiling, will speak of a "historic moment," of "durable peace," of "reconstruction" and "reconciliation." And you will still and forever be dead. As usual, it will be those who have killed or ordered killings who will have the privilege of celebrating the peace and being celebrated for having restored it. It will be both a day of solace and proof that they're all guilty, that the war was futile and useless, because too late, they'll have found a way to reconcile. On that day I will think of you, and I'll be ashamed for those who won't have the courage to be ashamed of themselves.

★★★

At the end of the ceremony, your grandmother and your father kiss you one last time. Your coffin is closed and you're transported a hundred metres farther on, to where you'll be buried. The firing continues. Each minute, we're a bit more fearful that it will be answered. I haven't even had time to reach the pit where you've been deposited, when I see everyone coming back along the snowy paths between the graves. The trucks armed with Grads pass by a second time. I can't see the faces of the soldiers inside. I'd have wanted to know what they look like, those men who press the buttons that sow death. I'd have wished to know something of their lives.

We leave the cemetery and go looking for what's left of your house. On Ilinskaya Street, a few dwellings bear the scars of recent bombardments. We park in front of the one that seems to have been yours. We've barely emerged from the car, when nearby firings bring us up short. Shells going out, therefore an imminent response. I have no time to confirm the address, just to take a few pictures. We leave immediately. As we came near we'd noticed, on the next street over, military vehicles and soldiers. Now it's all clear: rebel artillery is launching attacks on Ukrainian positions from your neighbourhood. The Ukrainians reply by shelling the area indiscriminately.

Looking at the photos later, I see, in the midst of the ruins, a green tricycle with yellow wheels. I imagine you on it a few days earlier.

★★★

Do you know what I did right after your funeral? I went to drink the best latte in town, at Jim's Coffee.

I went on with my life.

There I met a coffee importer. He told me about how hard it was to do business in these tough times. "The problem," he explained, "is less the war than the decline in the value of the hryvnia compared to the dollar." To each his catastrophes.

That evening I ate a pizza and drank a beer at a restaurant called The Mojito. It's on Artyom Street, Donetsk's main thoroughfare. It's named after Comrade Artyom, a Bolshevik hero who killed many people in the name of an ideology.

To kill: probably the best way to have a street named after you, one day.

Chapter 13

HATRED

A bus depot in the centre of Donetsk. A purple trolley bus with its windows blown out. Inside, a woman sweeps up death. She pushes bloodied water out the rear door. The snow turns red. On the benches, pieces of flesh. In her belly, hatred.

"Look! People were sitting here, and they're dead. And then they come and tell us that we're the terrorists? We're peaceful, hard-working people. We live in our houses, on our land. The terrorists are over there, in the west of Ukraine. Not here. Our comrade Sasha, the driver, was killed. He was driving people to work. Now his brain is all over the trolley bus. Go see for yourself in the trash can what we've already thrown out. And there's more. He earned money to feed his family. Was that being a terrorist? How can we bear that? Sasha had two children. Who's going to feed them now? Is Poroshenko going to feed them?"

A number of explosions are heard nearby.

"You hear? That's the kind of message we get from them. That's their humanitarian aid for Donbas! Every day we go to work under the bombs. You never know if you're going to get back alive. I've a four-year-old granddaughter. I don't know where to hide her so she'll be safe. You can't go out in the street to walk with a child. It's impossible to sleep, whether it's day or night. My greetings to western Ukraine! May God see to it that the same thing happens to their children. I hope their brains will explode too, and be scattered around. Our revenge will come one day. There's a God in this world. They're going to pay for all these deaths, for the deaths of our children. They say that we're their brothers. Where is that brotherhood they talk about? Son of a whore... My name is Irina Antashyuk. You can take my message to the media. I have relatives in western Ukraine. They tell me that we're firing on ourselves. I hope they'll see this. After that, let them say we're the terrorists. They'll see who's firing on whom."

Irina continues sweeping up blood while cursing Ukraine. There's no sadness in her voice. No compassion either. For her, justice arrives through vengeance.

★★★

A bus stop, Kuprin Street, in the south of the city. It's here, this morning, that the driver Sasha and seven of his passengers died, according to the account of the OSCE observers. The rebel authorities talk of thirteen victims, the same number as in the episode at Volnovakha. They blame the attack on "Ukrainian provocateurs" who infiltrated separatist territory and fired off mortars from a minibus.

Someone has placed a bouquet of flowers on the asphalt in front of the bus stop. The building opposite is riddled with pieces of shrapnel. The shopkeepers on the ground floor and the residents on the floors above are still boarding up their windows. A few dozen people are looking on. They're waiting for something, for somebody.

A convoy arrives. Aleksander Zakharchenko gets out of one of the vehicles. The DPR prime minister is quickly surrounded by passersby and journalists. Soon, a van filled with prisoners of war will appear. Zakharchenko wants the Ukrainian soldiers he's just captured to see what their fellows have done to the people of Donetsk. "You'll have a chance to look them in the eyes," he says to his people. An elderly woman speaks out.

- Can we also give them one on the mouth?
- Yes. But please don't kill them, as some have tried to do elsewhere.
- It wouldn't change much if we did kill them.
- I agree with you. They're animals. Poroshenko gave the order to shoot at will on Donetsk. He wants to scare the population.
- Give us one of them, at least!
- You want me to make you a present? I'll bring them to you.

The van arrives. A dozen men get out, dressed in rags, their clothes mismatched. They've been stripped of their military uniforms. They look less like soldiers than like sick and homeless people in distress. Some have bandaged heads or hands. Several have wounds on their faces. A few hours ago, these "cyborgs" were still hunkered down in the airport, under bullets and bombs. They saw their comrades die. They got out alive. They're the saved. But their suffering is not over. Now they must face the loathing of the population, must serve as scapegoats. They're paying in the name of Ukraine.

- American whores!
- Bastards!
- Murderers!

The crowd pelts them with snowballs and pieces of ice. The rebel soldiers shield them from the anger and vengefulness they themselves have encouraged.

A woman I'm trying to interview decides to vent her rage on me. I'm paying for the West.

- Your OSCE[18] doesn't see us as human. Europe and the United States don't want war on their territory, but here it suits them fine. They don't give a damn about the victims. You want people to see how we torture Ukrainian prisoners, is that it? You've found yourself a little show? Don't worry about them, no one's going to hurt

---

[18] The Organization for Security and Co-operation in Europe has a mandate to post observers in Ukraine. Its observers are unarmed civilians. It has no power to influence the military conduct of the war. It produces reports. Each of the member countries, including Russia, has a right of veto over its publications. The OSCE is present throughout Ukraine, but is powerless.

them. But when the bus passengers were killed, when the survivors were crying for help, where were you? Why didn't you report on that? Why don't you say what's going on here, with peaceful citizens being shot at?

- We see it and we talk about it.
- Who gives themselves the right to bomb peaceful people? Answer me! I live here, you live in Canada. Why are you shooting at me?
- I have no answer for that.
- Then for me that's already an answer. Your OSCE looks at us with empty eyes. It learned in Yugoslavia how to look at the dead.

★★★

Enough.

Enough of poisonous babushkas, ready to kill another woman's progeny;

> of humiliating dazed boys in public to excite a crowd's thirst for blood;
> of tank columns bolstering a belief in doing good through evil;
> of proud spiteful anger, shrill hatred, fingers on triggers;
> of rampant death posing as justice.

Enough. Of colleagues who peck away at the carrion, ask for leads, but refuse to share their own. Because *à la guerre comme à la guerre.* As if there weren't already enough sadness, mistrust, hypocrisy, traitorousness and lies to be had.

What do I want?

To defuse the hatred that lurks somewhere in each individual's tragedy;

for you not to be dead, Tyomochka;

for no one to be dead;

for me to have no photo of you in your coffin on my telephone;

for Anatoly Ivanovich to still be taking care of his vines and his grandson;

for Irina to be drinking tea with Sasha instead of scooping up his brain from the floor of the trolleybus;

for people to be talking about Shakhtar's next game while sipping coffee in the morning at Jim's Coffee, rather than about the growing violence and the arch enemy, as they clothe themselves in virtue.

They can say what they like, turn your body round every which way, war will never be pretty on anyone's face. Heroism is not superhuman, it's anti-human. Every victory is another defeat for our species.

In a few days, people will be calling to ask me what's happening in Donetsk. I'll no longer know. I'll be far from all that. I won't have forgotten anything. I'll just have stopped watching them playing their games. I'll just have stopped rubbing shoulders with hatred.

Chapter 14

LEAVING HATRED BEHIND

The buses won't be going to Mariupol today. What with the new passes the Ukrainian guards now almost routinely demand, rare are those who try to cross the front line, for fear of being turned back or never being able to return. Not counting the dangers: if ever they were delayed for too long in Volnovakha, would they risk being hit by a rocket like Anatoly Ivanovich's bus ten days ago?

Only one taxi driver allows a few people to share a ride as far as the last Ukrainian post, midway between Donetsk and Mariupol. From there, I hope to find other transportation.

One of the passengers talks about making the trip on a regular basis between the two large cities in the region, for his work. He still can't believe what is happening. Is it a bad dream, or does he really risk being arrested or being blown up by a bomb for those hundred kilometres of road that were once so banal and boring?

The last rebel roadblock. Our car will not go any farther. "The *Ukrops*[19] could be bombing from one moment to the next," warns a militiaman. We turn back and our driver stops near a bus stop. He gives us the choice. We can stay here and pray for an improbable bus to Mariupol, or return with him to Donetsk. We haven't had time to decide, when a multi-coloured van roars up and parks beside us. Heavily armed rebels get out. "You have no right to stop here." They demand our identity papers. My accreditation satisfies them. Those with a Ukrainian passport have to recite by heart the information set down in their passports. "Name, first name? Date of birth? Home address?" They search our bags, then let us go.

Back at the station, just as I'm resigning myself to being stuck one more day in Donetsk, a bus driver walks by, calling out "Mariupol! Mariupol!" He tells me that he plans to leave the highway a bit before Volnovakha and take smaller roads cross-country, where the controls are not so strict. At Vugledar, a farming village, another bus will be waiting to get us back on the highway beyond Volnovakha, then to Mariupol. The detour through the countryside will take several hours. But at least, we should get there.

And the worst will be behind us at last.

---

[19] "Dill." A nickname given to Ukrainian soldiers thanks to its resemblance to "*Ukr*," short for the word "Ukrainian."

FRÉDÉRICK LAVOIE

★★★

To leave hatred behind
along cross-country roads
gazing on landscapes
of ice fishing
still lifes

above all
don't prove the vultures right
don't feed
on venomous smiles
on shattered silences
on shrapnel in the cheeks of others

above all
don't become
the snake's golden tongue
or the falcon's evil eye
do not stake
a single retort
on the perfidious lottery
resist
the irreparable

return to what grows
to the boom boom
of elated children
running upstairs

to grandmothers
who cry out for no reason
to the sparrows' skies
to the wind in our backs

bring back
an attainable goodness
harmony

on the horizon

***

Mariupol, at nightfall. The city has known no war for five months, ever since the Ukrainian forces drove out the rebels. Here I am far from violence. At least, so I think.

Chapter 15

CORNERED AGAIN

Friends, allies, peacemakers, bestowers of tenderness, are there to greet me on the other side of hatred. We drink, we sing. Over the loudspeakers, Olga Arefyeva spews venom on the bombs along with us:

> To hell with war
> let it go and screw itself!
>
> Enough of always building on the ruins
>
> Enough of the bloody battle for peace
>
> To hell with war
> let it go and screw itself!

★★★

Twenty after nine, the next morning. The walls of the house start trembling, violently. Thirty seconds, then nothing. Confirmation that the worst has happened arrives a few minutes later through the local media. A Grad attack has struck a neighbourhood in the east of the city, a dozen kilometres from where I am, behind the huge wall of steel mills that looms on the horizon. The dead are quickly counted in the dozens.

I came to Mariupol because I'd had enough of this filthy war. Now it's catching up with me. I'd like to ignore it, but I can't. I can't bring myself to turn my back, not *to go and see what there is to see*, to take the measure of the devastation in order to bear witness. I'm probably the only foreign correspondent in the city. All the others are in the midst of the conflict, in Donetsk, Luhansk, Debaltseve. Mariupol has been outside it all for months.

It takes me two hours to decide, to wait for another attack or a reply to it. Nothing happens. I call a taxi. No need for an address. Once I get near to the approximate site of the attack, the smoking ruins guide me. The taxi drops me off in front of Yasny Lane. There I meet Oksana. Her guest house, recently built in her garden, has been torn to shreds by a shell. Fortunately, there was no one inside. Oksana doesn't want to speculate on the origins of the attack. Her neighbour Yevgeny has no doubts: "It came from the east, of course. We're eleven kilometres from Shirokino, where these kind souls are positioned. What weapons are they using, you ask? Russian weapons. I don't think, I know. They're the ones who supply these drunks, these rebel bandits. They've decided to send us a weekend present to destabilize the situation here. Mariupol is the only city in the region that's been functioning normally for the last while. As long as Russia is supplying the rebels, this conflict will never end. Russia doesn't want a successful Ukraine."

A rocket shell is standing upright in Yevgeny's yard. He's getting ready to cover the windows of his house with plastic sheeting. It will be unliveable for the rest of the winter. Afterwards, he'll see what he can do. The war has cost him his job in an orphanage, shut down since the hostilities began. Now, it's stolen his house. His daughter barely escaped with her life. This morning's attack riddled her bedroom with shrapnel from the missile. "When I saw the first rockets falling on the Kyivsky Market, I went to grab her and pushed her into the kitchen. Otherwise she'd be dead, that's certain."

I continue my inspection of the neighbourhood. Many buildings have been affected, some partly destroyed. The firemen are fighting the flames eating away at a toy store. In a parking lot, the carcasses of about fifteen cars are smoking, beside a crater where the tip of a rocket has buried itself. Near the site's shelter is the lot's owner. He was in the same spot this morning at the time of the attack. "I didn't see anything, I was looking down. I fell, and I stayed on the ground." His hand is scraped from the fall, his ears are buzzing, but otherwise he's fine. About a dozen metres from there, another rocket, however, has planted itself in the asphalt. If it had fallen two or three metres farther back, the flying shrapnel would probably not have spared him. As for the first rocket, which cost him his parking lot, he was protected from it by his shelter's sheet metal wall. The difference between life and death was for him just a matter of a few metres and a law of physics.

I take a look at the craters. There's no doubt: the warheads came from the east, the rebel territories, as Yevgeny assured us. Not surprising. Mariupol is under the control of the government. The rebels want to retake it. They're the ones who are firing indiscriminately. Like the Ukrainians onto your neighbourhood six days ago, Tyomochka. In either case, I can't believe that civilians were the target. Maybe I'm wrong. Maybe there's an evil plan to kill innocents, and to deplete the morale of the enemy camp. I prefer to assume that the bombings in residential areas are, rather, a sign of the extraordinary incompetence of the artillerymen, plus a criminal indifference on the part of the belligerents to human life.

A few isolated mortar firings resonate in the distance. I spot people who have taken refuge in an apartment building's basement. It's the only bomb shelter available. Inside, I find pacifists caught in a trap. They've been cowering in the shadows since morning. "We're like hostages here. Hostages both of Ukraine and the rebels," says Anatoly, an engineer who speaks in a calm voice. The retiree Maria Vasiliyevna adds: "The representatives of the Popular Republic of Donetsk and those of the Ukraine government are going to have to come to some sort of agreement, so there won't be any more victims. They have to make peace. Because all this is no good for anyone. They ought to reflect a little, to have empathy for the people, and understand that this has to stop. I'm seventy-six years old. At my age, if something happens to me, I don't so much care. But I'm sad for the children, the young people." Anatoly's and Maria's feelings of impotence and helplessness are both sad and reassuring. There are still people who are seeking neither victory nor vengeance. Only an end to the war.

I come out of the basement. I've barely gone a few metres when a Grad breaks the silence. I go back below ground, to Anatoly and Maria. It's 1:02 PM. It's been four hours since the first attack. This new firing seems to have struck far from the neighbourhood.

I'm not here to risk my life. This bombing reminds me of that.

I decide, all the same, to go and check out the state of the Kyivsky Market, apparently the place hardest hit by this morning's assault. Just one more bit of bravado before leaving.

Across what was once the market wall, I spot Aleksander wading through the debris of his computer store. He helps me to scramble inside.

- I don't know what happened. I can't tell you why the rocket fell here. The market opens a bit before nine o'clock, but most of the merchants arrive later. Fortunately, my employee wasn't early.

- What are you going to do now that your store has been destroyed?

- Live. Keep on living. I've nothing any more. No insurance. No one insures anyone now anyway because of the war. And even if I had it, I don't think I'd be compensated. In a country like ours, they always find a way to leave you in the lurch. What's important is to be alive. Everything I worked for during all those years…

Aleksander doesn't have time to finish his sentence. A new series of staccato firings sets the sky to trembling. Grads again. A few kilometres from here, someone has pressed a button and forty rockets have flown off. The roar seems to suggest that they're headed our way.

You know the rest, Tyoma: the empty stall, my ill-informed hesitations, me in a little ball in the middle of the room, awaiting the worst.

Then nothing. Luck. Life.

After that, the abnormal quickly goes back to normal in the market. Either the shopkeepers excel in the art of hiding their emotions, or they're fatalists who give that impression while they're taking stock of the ruins. For myself, I've had enough. Too much. I didn't want that much. On the way back, I curse myself. I find myself stupid *a posteriori* for having risked my life, even a little bit. Nothing happened. But anything could have happened. I had no control over the firing buttons on the Shirokino Grads. I'm not traumatized, but I'm far from proud. I'll never allow myself to tell this tale with a silly smile. I don't play that game. I'm neither cat nor mouse. I'm a white flag.

Nakhrena nam voina, poshla ona na!

To hell with war, let it go and screw itself!

By the end of the day, the count has reached thirty

dead and a hundred wounded. From his hospital bed, the welder Sergey sums up the philosophy of the white flag:

"It's the war that fired on us."

He'd asked for nothing, but he'd received it anyway. This time from one side, the next time, perhaps, from the other.

★★★

Two days later there are burials at Novotroitskoye, a grey and depressing cemetery in the shadow of the steel mills. Larissa, a sixty-six-year-old retired engineer, is laid in the ground. At about 9:20 AM on Saturday, rocket shrapnel had attained her vital organs. "She was a Ukraine patriot, she went to the roadblocks to bring food to the soldiers," her friend Luba tells me. Larissa's son gets angry when he sees the cameras. He damages one. During the months of calm, Mariupol had enough time to lose its warlike reflexes. It doesn't want anyone to capitalize on its deaths. If the conflict ends up putting down roots again in the city, attitudes will change, certainly. But for now, the refusal to take sides provides grounds for optimism. People are still hoping that Saturday's attacks will remain an anomaly, and that no one will have to clothe himself again in hatred and choose one side.

That same day, I leave Mariupol, without waiting to see whether the conflict will settle in once more.

Chapter 16

A FATHER IN MOURNING

He comes into the café and holds out one of his large hands, so large that he feels impelled to draw attention to their disproportion with mine. We sit down and order drinks.

"I'm going to explain to you why my son found himself on Greek Square in Odessa on May 2, 2014."

That was nine months ago. The darkest and most contentious day in Odessa's modern history. The darkest day of Luka Losinsky's life.

That afternoon, two concurrent demonstrations, pro- and anti-Maidan, are taking place in the city centre. The verbal confrontation quickly becomes a physical clash: a few punches and blows from sticks, a few stones thrown, then some gunshots that end with a handful of dead and wounded. The anti-Maidan camp, fewer in numbers, takes refuge in the Trade Unions Building. The fighting continues. Molotov cocktails and other projectiles are exchanged from inside the building to the outside and from outside to inside. The police are powerless. A fire breaks out. Most of the militants are able to escape, sometimes with the help of their adversaries, who see that there's a disaster in the making. Other anti-Maidan supporters are trapped on the upper floors. They die asphyxiated, burned, or in jumping from windows to flee the flames. More than forty victims, all told.

Zhenya, Mister Losinsky's son, was one of the first to be wounded, shot when the two demonstrations came together. He died in the hospital nine days later.

★★★

"That was the first time he had taken part in such an event. He was on the anti-Maidan side. Why did he get involved? You see, both of Zhenya's grandparents fought during the Second World War. The first, my father, defended Odessa. He was in the Soviet navy. He volunteered at the age of seventeen. When he was wounded and was released from the army, he stayed anyway and joined the ranks of the partisans against the fascists. His war ended in Hungary, in 1946. As for his maternal grandfather, he fought in Leningrad, and then participated in the taking of Berlin. For Zhenya, the Second World War was sacred. He adored his grandfathers. Together, we took part in historical reconstructions of the great battles. On April 10th, we celebrated the day of Odessa's liberation. May 9th was the day of Victory. And August 4th marked the anniversary of the day when Odessa's defence began. For him, it was a very serious exercise. Some people dressed up as German soldiers, and we were in Soviet uniforms.

Zhenya knew this history well. He'd studied it. He was very moved by the stories of those people who had sacrificed their lives to defend the world against fascism. During the celebrations, we wore the black and orange ribbon of Saint George. Today, the rebels of Donetsk and Luhansk have also made it their symbol. Many now think it's a symbol of separatism. But in the beginning, this ribbon united the Soviet peoples who had vanquished the Nazi enemy. Without the struggle represented by this ribbon, there would be no Ukraine, not even any Russia. There would only be a great fascist Germany. It mustn't be forgotten that we conquered the Nazis first, and only then were we able to build Ukraine. Zhenya was wearing the ribbon when he went to Greek Square. He didn't like it that the new government was imposing the cult of Stepan Bandera and Roman Shukhevych, the Ukrainian nationalists who had fought alongside the SS. That said, when you think about it, their combat was not so very different from that of today's separatists in Donetsk and Luhansk. Those nationalists were part of a minority that fought for freedom against an oppressive central power. They weren't seeking to take someone else's territory. Like the people in Donetsk and Luhansk now, they wanted their independence and collaborated with an occupying power in hopes of obtaining it at the end of the line. You can't use different criteria to judge Bandera's sympathizers at the time, and today's separatists. Either you say they're all bad, or you say they're all good. I've nothing against recognizing Bandera and the others as heroes of Western

Ukraine, where they fought. Many people have a grandfather who participated in the movement, and they want to honour him. That's fine. Let everyone have his heroes. I won't go to Ternopil to destroy a statue of Bandera. But why stop me from waving the red Soviet flag during celebrations? Why do they want to destroy the monuments honouring my heroes, my ancestors? Zhenya was claiming the right to keep waving that flag. He refused to let them stop him from living as we've always lived. He didn't want them to force him to adopt others' heroes as his own. He wanted Odessa to remain Odessa. Here, we greet each other, saying *"Zdravstvuitye"* in Russian, *"Shalom"* in Yiddish, and *"Dobrovo dnya"* in Ukrainian. Now, many public events, like the sessions at the city hall, begin with a "Glory to Ukraine! To the heroes, glory!" That's the motto of Ukrainian nationalists during the Second World War. Why do they want to force us to prove our patriotism by greeting each other with such phrases? It's because of that that Zhenya went to demonstrate on Greek Square.

"I believe that if he was killed, it's because he stood out. Many demonstrators wore Second World War helmets, but he wore his costume from the medieval tournament. We also participated in reconstructions of fourteenth century tournaments. He had a helmet with a visor, armour, a wooden shield, and a rubber club. There's a photo of him, taken five minutes before he was shot. You see him, sitting on the sidewalk, his shield beside him. He spent the whole demonstration defending his friends, and even people he didn't know, against the stones and bottles being tossed at them. He attacked no one, all he did was defend. I don't mean to say he was perfect. He went there to fight, just like the others. He was a maximalist. When you're young, you often see things in black and white. On one of the videos, you see Zhenya in the front row. Then the camera turns, and you see a man, his face masked, shooting in his direction with a hunting rifle. He fires four times. He was the only person with a weapon on the square. Zhenya was hit by a number of pellets.

"Five hundred people came to his funeral. Yet he wasn't a hero, or a famous journalist, or some kind of public figure. He was an ordinary boy, an Odessan. Among those who were there, there were anti-Maidans, but also pro-Maidans. No one saw him as a separatist, or anything of the sort. They loved him, that's all. Zhenya was not just my son. He was also my friend and my business partner. We had a spice importation business. We went regularly to Madagascar, to Tanzania, to Kenya. In fact he'd just come back from four months in Madagascar. We participated in historical reconstructions together, we did diving and horseback riding together. We went hunting and fishing. We shared the same opinions. To lose my son was very painful. But I'm not ashamed of the way he died. He went out into the street to defend his ideas. It's not right that he died like that. My son adored Ukraine. He had friends everywhere in the country. He wanted a democratic Ukraine, a state that respected the rule of law. Sadly, that state does not yet exist. He died for that.

"I looked at all the videos I could find, to understand what happened. That's how we found the probable murderer. His name is Sergey Khodiak. I can't say he's the killer, because I believe in justice and the presumption of innocence. But there is damaging evidence against him. Khodiak was at all the demonstrations. We sent the police all the proof we gathered. Two days later, he was arrested. He was already known in the criminal world. He was also a member of the ultranationalist group Pravy Sektor. When he was in detention, his friends came to the prison with tires and Molotov cocktails and demanded that he be released, supposedly because he was arrested illegally. The authorities took him out through a back entrance, and brought him to Kyiv. At his trial there, 150 people came to put pressure on the judge. Khodiak was placed under house arrest, but after six months, according to law, he had to be released. Now he walks free without being bothered by anybody. My understanding is that he'll never have to go on trial. If he appears, a few hundred of his supporters will come and protest, saying they're prosecuting a hero, a nationalist who fought for Odessa and for Ukraine. In an interview, he himself said that his case ought not to be judged by investigators and judges, but by Ukraine patriots. It's absurd. The law ought to be the same for everybody. On the Internet, you can find many people saying that he and the others responsible for the May 2nd tragedy shouldn't be judged, because they saved Odessa from a scenario similar to that of Donetsk, and Luhansk. For them, the death of forty-seven people put an end to the separatist inclinations of some, and kept the peace in the city.

"If it were my son or another anti-Maidan who had killed someone, everything would have gone differently. They would have been quickly judged and condemned. Today, the anti-Maidans are considered enemies of the state. The government is blaming Russian involvement for the May 2nd events. The same thing for the bomb attacks these days in Odessa, which curiously never make any victims. If the Russians really wanted to do damage, they have plenty of experts who could organize really murderous attacks. They'd probably blow up bridges, to cut Odessa off from the rest of the country. I think it's actually the powers that be that organize these terrorist attacks to justify sending troops into the city. It's easier to control the masses by pointing your finger at an outside enemy. Understand me. I don't in any way support the Russian occupation of Ukraine, or Putin. On the other hand, I think that, in ninety per cent of the cases, this outside enemy we're supposed to believe in is imaginary. As long as there's war in Donetsk, as long as we're fighting a so-called enemy, no one is going to demand that the government be accountable. No one is going to ask it why the country is getting poorer day by day. The truth is, we're all to blame for what's happening to us. In twenty-five years of independence, we haven't been able to build a thing. We only think about destroying, eliminating. Before, there were big factories everywhere. They don't exist any more. Why are we putting all our energy into dismantling statues of Lenin, instead of building factories? An entire generation has been lost. Excuse me, but today the girls only think about becoming prostitutes, and the boys, bandits. Many parents have opted not to educate their children. And despite all that, the nationalists tell the young that they're better than other people. It's like in Germany in the 1930s, with the Aryan race. Today, the simple fact of belonging to the Ukrainian race is supposed to be a sign of superiority. No need to read, to study, or to work, we're already the best, while the Russians are just drunkards and criminals!

"I'm a fourth-generation Odessan. I don't have to prove to anyone that I belong to this city and this country. I adore Ukraine. My father is Ukrainian born. I don't want Russia, I don't want a federalization of the country. I think we can see to our own needs. We have resources. But our misfortune is that this revolution only swept thieves from power, to install other thieves. The Maidan rose up because Yanukovych no longer wanted to ally himself with Europe. Some only needed a pretext like that to overthrow him by force. If we'd waited eight months, there would have been a presidential election. And we could have voted for someone else. The revolution created a precedent. It showed that with stones, Molotov cocktails, and weapons, you could grab power. Since then, the Pandora's box has been opened. If you can do that in Kyiv, why not in Donetsk or Luhansk? I think this war was started intentionally. Why was one of the first laws adopted after the revolution, one concerning official languages? Why do that? Why didn't someone say: "A new Ukraine has risen. We are all brothers and sisters, from north to south, Let's work together!" Many members of parliament are prosperous businessmen. They're not stupid. They figured that they had to propose this law to foment the war.

"I remember the first death on the Maidan. It was a national tragedy. Everyone wept. Today, they routinely announce the death of ten or twenty civilians on the same day. And we consider that normal. Nobody weeps any more. Not only that, the victims are regarded differently, depending on whether they've died in the separatist zone or that under Ukrainian control. When a bus is blown up by an explosion in Volnovakha, it's a national day of mourning. But when the passengers of a trolleybus are killed in Donetsk, we do nothing. Yet all these people are supposed to be our citizens. We claim that it's our territory. So why the double standard? No one asks these kinds of questions.

"When Yanukovych withdrew from the association agreement with the European Union, Zhenya and I thought that it was the wrong decision. We knew that we had to get closer to Europe. But at the same time, we knew that we also had to maintain our relations with Russia. For the time being, Ukraine cannot survive without Russia. Our level of development is closer to that of Russia than that of the Europeans. The idea of joining Europe is unrealistic today. Many Ukrainians work over there, but with their hands, in restaurants or on construction sites. Europe has no need of starving barbarians like us. We have to start building infrastructures here, to adapt to European norms. I consider myself an educated man. I often go to Europe. I'm used to not paying for parking, for example, just leaving my car anywhere. I'm not ready to be a European. Ukraine is not ready either.

"Under Yanukovych, things were very bad. Now, they're even worse. Except that when he was in power there was no war, no separatist regions. Ukrainians were not dying at the front. Crimea was Ukrainian. I could go there with my family. Yanukovych was a thief. He and his clan of oligarchs laid their hands on all of the country's wealth. Most Ukrainians detested him. But the dollar was at eight hryvnias. A retired person received two hundred dollars a month. A new regime took his place. The dollar fell to twenty-two, twenty-three hryvnias. The oligarchs are still in parliament. Today, everyone is afraid of tomorrow. Everyone says, 'This is bad, but let's pray that it stays like that, so it won't get even worse.'

"In Africa, Zhenya and I filled containers with spices to ship them to the port of Odessa. We then sold them in bulk. The new government has just imposed a retroactive tax on imports. With the fluctuation of the dollar, the loss of our clients in the separatist regions and in Crimea, and the decline in buying power, the business is no longer viable. From now to the end of the year, I'll probably have to shut down the company. I don't see any light at the end of the tunnel. I'm fifty-eight years old. I raised a marvellous son. I have a three-and-a-half-year-old girl,

Taisa. Zhenya's daughter, Masha, is eleven. I don't see any future for them in Ukraine. They're taking intensive courses in English. I want them to go and study in Lithuania, in Canada, in England. Anywhere, but not in Ukraine. There's nothing to do here. People earn barely fifty dollars a month. They say it's because of the war, of Putin. Yes, Putin is partly the cause, but so are we.

"I dream of my son every night. Sometimes I forget where I've put papers, or what I've done with my keys, but I can describe to you in detail every scene from these dreams. In every one, I see him alive, never dead. He smiles at me. On the one hand, it's wonderful to be able to *meet* my son each night, but on the other, it's a sorrow forever revived."

★★★

Luka Losinsky pays the bill before I can pull out my wallet. He goes off with his grief, his resilience, and the strong conviction that as long as the victors of the revolution deny their part of the responsibility for the current tragedy, Ukraine's fragmentation will only go on.

Chapter 17

THE BLIND SPOT

Back in Kyiv, I meet the cream of the Ukrainian intelligentsia. If I lived here, Tyoma, I'd hope to count these people among my acquaintances or even friends. They're young, intelligent, cultivated, connected, learned, honest, open to the world. They speak foreign languages, they travel, they write books. They sparked the revolution, and continue to fight to do away with the corruption that poisons the economy of your country and the minds of your citizens. They aren't trying to enrich themselves personally by taking advantage of their positions. They believe in justice, equity, democracy, individual liberty, and want every Ukrainian to be able to take advantage of it all as much as they do themselves. I could listen to them for hours, discussing and debating over a glass of wine or beer, looking for solutions to reinvent the state and to extricate it from its post-Soviet inertia. They are the incarnation of what the Revolution of Dignity has, at its best, brought to Ukraine. They are the hope for true change, and the vibrant force that is working to make it real.

And yet.

As soon as I bring up the subject of the causes of your death, of the war in Donbas, and the alienation of its inhabitants, they put on their blinkers. Suddenly they're intransigent, Manichaean, even ignorant. Their indignation becomes selective. Their capacity for empathy, discernment, and self-criticism stops where the front line begins, there where the territorial integrity of *their* country is called into question.

★★★

Iryna Slavinska is a journalist, translator, author, and radio host. In a Kyiv café she talks to me at length about what, in her opinion, constitutes the most significant success of the revolution: the creation of a genuine civil society. Enthusiastically, she tells me how tens of thousands of your fellow citizens have spontaneously given their time and energy to build a new Ukraine. They have done so independently of political parties, and without waiting for any material benefit from this involvement. "These are horizontal movements, without any hierarchy. Those who began by working in the Maidan kitchens, for example, now send food to soldiers in the combat zones. It's the kind of benevolent activity that will endure beyond the war, I'm sure of that." Within the ministries, she explains, citizens' groups act as deterrents to people in power, preventing bureaucrats from going back to their old ways of doing things. They force them to answer to the public. Ukraine has risen, and has no intention of let-ting the revolution be overthrown again. And so much the better.

Iryna has participated in these successes. She is confident. In fact, she believes that were it not for the "Russian invasion," post-revolutionary Ukraine would be united, and nothing could stop its advancement towards Europe. For her, there is no other explanation for the fragmentation of the country than this external enemy.

"This conflict with Donbas was artificial from the start. In the beginning, the demands of the anti-Maidan protestors were social in nature. Their leaders said they were against the oligarchs and were defending the miners and retired persons. They didn't talk about the Russian language. Okay, maybe a little, but the general idea was that life would be better if an imaginary Putin came to raise the old-age pensions and people' salaries.But in any case, the day a foreign army invades a city, the language law has nothing more to do with what's going on."

For Iryna, the fears of the Russian speakers in the east and in Crimea were and remain hollow. After all, she reminds me, the ultranationalists who were trying to restrict their rights have always been a tiny minority, and won only a handful of seats in the new parliament. The abolition of the language law was not ratified by the interim president. It's Russian propaganda that inflamed that issue. The Kremlin wanted to undermine the revolution and divide the country so that the regions it coveted would fall into its hands like ripe fruit.

Iryna is not paranoid. She's right when she says that

the Russian speakers' greatest fears with regard to the new government have not materialized. The voices of reason, in the end, prevailed over those of the extremists. But what she does not realize is that no one took it upon himself to go to Donbas and to Crimea to diminish this largely unfounded mistrust. No one tried to build any bridges. It's less the disagreements themselves that triggered the crisis, than the lack of communication. The victors were arrogant. A simple dialogue, or even a monologue on their part, would have shown that the majority opinions on each side were not as far apart as some - the Russian propagandists in particular - wanted people to believe.

Iryna cannot see where the revolution has failed. She cannot grasp how two solitudes can interpret differently the same events, and each others' intentions. Yet she is not the sort of person to evade difficult issues. If there are people in Kyiv who ought to have been able to heed the complaints in the east and Crimea, it's certainly Iryna and her colleagues. On the radio, they criticize the poor decisions of those now in power, as much as they celebrate their good works. They're at the forefront of post-revolutionary change. They elevate the debate to a very high level. And open the floor to the representatives of all social and political factions. But when the time comes to speak of the war, to try to understand and to explain it, their minds shut down. "We don't give air time to terrorists," Iryna asserts. Whether it be a rebel leader or a grandmother who's distraught as a result of Ukrainian bombings, they don't want to know. As a matter of principle, they wouldn't listen to your father blaming Ukrainian forces for your death. They don't want to know his reasoning, to understand how he could go from neutrality to hatred of Kyiv thanks to a missile carelessly launched against his home. The separatists and all those who support them, near and far, are evil. Your father is evil.

Like most Ukrainians, Iryna will consider this conflict ended only when the army has retaken the territories now in the hands of rebels. But if this day arrives, the government will have to persuade all the Ukrainian citizens who found themselves either by choice or against their will on the wrong side of the front line, to forgive it for having bombed them for months in order to "liberate" them; it will have to convince your parents to forgive it for having killed you, swearing that there was no other solution, and that there's still a place for them in this reunified Ukraine.

For the moment, that prospect seems remote. And Iryna prefers to contribute to the war effort rather than to prepare the ground for a reconciliation.

- When Ukrainian firings kill civilians, do you mention it on the radio?

- The Ukrainian army says that it only shoots as a response. When we talk about bombings, we state the names of the villages where they took place, and the number of victims. From the newsroom in Kyiv, I can't verify the exact origins of the firing. When I'm a newsreader, I prefer not to lie. I don't provide information I don't know.

- Do you react in the same way in the opposite case? Have you said, for example, that the attack on Mariupol was a terrorist attack, or that the origins of the firing were undetermined?

- When you're on air the day of an attack, it's hard not to use the word "terrorist." I've done it. I've often characterized the rebels as terrorists. But that's my personal opinion. In our newsroom, we have no rule on the subject.

I'd like to be able to say that Iryna, the kind Iryna, the brilliant Iryna, is as much offended by your death as by that of Anatoly Ivanovich in the bus at Volnovakha. I'd like to tell you that she thought even for a second that the end did not justify all means. But no. She did as you do in a war. She stared straight ahead, without throwing a glance at the blind spot of her convictions, and she continued to hate those to whom she refused to listen.

I know, Tyoma, I'm being hard on Iryna, but that's because if there's any hope for peace, it must come from people like her, rather than the brutes who take pleasure in lobbing bombs at others' houses.

★★★

Sitting in an Italian restaurant in the middle of town, Serhiy Leshchenko spends more than an hour scribbling figures and faces on his tablemat. He explains to me in great detail how Yanukovych, along with his clan, orchestrated the division of Ukraine for political ends during the last decade. For years, the former investigative journalist for *Ukrainska Pravda* has been trying to bring to light his power-grabbing ploys, and to denounce his ties with Moscow. A few months after the revolution, he entered politics in order to ensure that the changes he'd longed for so desperately would in fact materialize. In other words, he threw his hat in the ring for the right reasons. "I don't like politics. As a deputy, I earn 4,846 hryvnias per month. That comes out to 300 dollars. Politics is not lucrative if it isn't corrupt." Since his election to parliament, Serhiy has been fighting against corruption, uncovering the schemes of the oligarchs close to power, and attacking abuses of all sorts. He has at his fingertips all of the country's vital political dossiers. Except for the conflict in the east. On this subject, his reasoning may be reduced to one word: Putin. Like Iryna, he rejects any likelihood that the disaffection on the part of the populace in these regions stems from the parliament's unforgiving decisions in the first post-revolutionary hours.

At the end of the interview, the former journalist reverses our roles, and starts questioning me on the subject of my time in separatist territory. He has not visited Donbas for years, and he's now forbidden to set foot there. "So how is it there? Where did this Zakharchenko come from, anyway? What does he want, exactly? A federation? Autonomy?" Serhiy knows that the war is of vital importance to the future of his country. But clearly, he hasn't been that interested in it up to now. He's been busy building a new Ukraine, a state whose existence - or at least whose territorial integrity - is, all the same, directly threatened by what's going on in the east. For him, the war is a separate problem. Even if it's happening within the country's borders, and even if it involves millions of its citizens, he's treating it as if it were an external point of contention between Ukraine and Russia.

***

Two days later, when the historian Volodymyr Vyatrovich tells me that "Ukrainians are more divided by the myths surrounding their history than by their history itself," I feel, briefly, as if I've found a voice of reason. The director of the Institute of National Memory is well placed to know that, in a conflict, different versions of the past are weapons that must be handled with care, justifications for everything and its opposite. But quickly, I see that like the others, he prefers to wield his weapon rather than to denounce its misuse. "Take Stepan Bandera. In the east, they say that he collaborated with the Nazis, but he was for a long time interned in Nazi camps. They say he was an anti-Semite, which is just a Soviet invention. On the other side, there's the comrade Artyom. He was a Bolshevik terrorist who fought against the Ukrainian state. We can't accept that he be recognized as a hero, even at the local level, and that a street in Donetsk continue to bear his name."

Volodymyr actively participated in Euromaidan. Under the old regime, he lost his job at the National Archives. For those clinging to the status quo, he was making too many waves. In the aftermath of the revolution, he was named director of the institute. His predecessor under Yanukovych was "an old Communist who did everything by the book," he says. Now it's his turn to do everything as it should be done. Ukraine had its heroes: Soviets who had killed Ukrainians or who'd had them killed. Volodymyr's task is to replace them with others: nationalists who have also killed Ukrainians or had them killed.

★★★

Among the intellectuals I meet in Kyiv, only one acknowledges the revolution's blind spot. "Right after Yanukovych's overthrow, the new leaders should have made a symbolic journey to Donbas to reassure the people. There, the revolution was not understood." The political analyst Maria Zolkina is as fervent as the others in her support of Euromaidan. She spent days and nights on the square, demanding a new Ukraine. What sets her apart from the others: she's from Luhansk. She knows her native city should have been listened to, and its trust won, to avoid its feeling threatened by the new power and its nationalist tendencies. And she saw right away that this was not a priority for the victors.

★★★

In the Centre for the Study of Public Policy, between an analysis of the conflict's impact on the economy and the prospects for Ukrainian industry's integration with the

European market, the economist Vasil Povoroznyk unconsciously puts his finger on another sore spot: "When the people in Donbas say that we're not listening to them, they forget that they were in power during the four years of Yanukovych's rule. During that time, they were the only people the regime listened to." There, it's said. The revolutionaries' indifference to the demands of their fellow citizens was nothing but an act of revenge. A revenge that was perhaps satisfying at the time, but that is today taking its toll on everyone.

★★★

You can rarely count on the military to call things into question. Igor Lapin was a soldier in the Soviet army, then the Russian, and finally the Ukrainian. He then practised law for seventeen years. When the east ignited, he took up arms once more in the Aidar battalion, one of the popular militias that acted as adjunct forces to the regular army. His heroism won him an election as a deputy in 2014. I interview him in the hall of parliament, during a pause in the current session.

- What can be done to end the conflict?
- Stop the aggressor. Fight, what else? Some thought it would be enough to abandon Crimea to the Russians, and then things would calm down. Have they calmed down? They've spread to Donetsk and Luhansk. If we let things go, soon they'll come all the way to Kyiv.

\- What do you think about the people who've stayed in the separatist zones?

\- Some people are so attached to their material possessions that they refuse to leave. They're ready to live in a basement, knowing that their house can be bombed at any time. Those who support the separatists are in another category. They are traitors to our country. They're counting on Russia to save them. Then there's a last category; those who don't even know that the government will help them if they want to flee. I'm sorry for them.

\- Then how can you convince them to leave or to rise up against the rebels?

\- We must cut off their lifeline. Stop paying pensions and salaries. Because people with full stomachs don't revolt. If they've nothing to eat, they'll take up arms against the separatists. There's no other way.

Starve innocent people so they'll revolt. That's what your country has come to, Artyom. Never mind if this strategy has so often proved to be counterproductive; never mind that wherever it has been used, it has, rather, induced people to support the power in place, the only one continuing to feed it.

The stick is tempting. It seems more effective than the carrot. But torture rarely inspires fondness in the victim.

Chapter 18

ON THE UNPREDICTABILITY OF THE PAST

A Saturday morning in February, in the Lychakiv Cemetery in Lviv, far to the country's west. A few families are gathered in front of mounds of earth covered with wreaths of flowers. "Zhenya...Zhenya..." moans a woman, walking away from the photo of the soldier who was probably her husband. Since the beginning of the hostilities in the east, the old cemetery has seen thirty or so new military graves added to the hundreds that were there already. There is still room for many more.

The front is more than a thousand kilometres from here. The bombs don't reach Lviv. But over the months, thousands from Lviv have travelled to where the bombs are. Volunteers in battalions or conscripts in the regular army, they've gone to defend *their* Ukraine against the foreign invasion and the country's collapse. Many of them began their fight on the Maidan. They went there to hold placards, then bricks, stones, sticks, Molotov cocktails, and ultimately, guns. Some of the more radical revolutionaries were from Lviv, the cradle of Ukrainian nationalism. When the situation became inflamed in Donbas, going to the front was for them just the logical extension of their commitment. Since then many have come back to the West, feet first. In the part of the cemetery reserved for the *Defenders of Lviv*, a new section has been opened for them.

In theory, these patriots ought to have the honour of lying in Lychakiv forever, beside other heroes who made their mark on the city's history. But we can never be certain of what the future holds in wait for the dead of past wars. This cemetery knows something about that. In its twenty-three decades of existence, it's seen it all: burial, exhumation, profanation, reburial, destruction, reconstruction. That's what happens when you find yourself, as in Lviv, at the crossroads of empires. Those in the ascendant at a particular time hold sway not only over your present, but also your past. They decide which dead to honour and which ones to forget.

When the Poles retook Lviv at the end of the First World War, they removed the Austro-Hungarian soldiers' graves in order to bury their own men killed during the re-conquest. At the end of the Second World War, when the Soviets "liberated" the city, the Polish soldiers were in turn dislodged from Lychakiv. Their graves were razed, and the site turned into a truck depot. When Ukraine became independent, those now in power did not do away with the gravestones of the Red Army soldiers, but they stripped them of any suggestion of glory. The partisans of Stepan Bandera's Ukrainian Insurgent Army, which had battled the Soviets, were finally given space in the cemetery.

Today, among the *Defenders of Lviv*, we find a few hundred cement crosses perfectly aligned. They are recent, even if all the inscribed death dates fall between 1918 and 1920. A plaque explains this paradox:

> We, Presidents of Ukraine and the Republic of Poland, in inaugurating this monument commemorating the soldiers of the Ukrainian Army of Galicia and the graves of the Polish soldiers of the years 1918-1920 in the Lychakiv cemetery, seek to reaffirm Ukraine-Polish harmony in the name of a shared European home, and we solemnly proclaim the historical reconciliation and the understanding between our peoples.
>
> President of Ukraine
> *Viktor Yushchenko*
> President of the Republic of Poland
> *Aleksander Kwaśniewski*
>
> June 24, 2005

It took a decade and a half of post-Communism in the two countries for them to agree on some semblance of a shared past. Between 1918 and 1920, there were two wars in Galicia. First, the Ukrainians, seeking to profit from the fall of the Austro-Hungarian Empire to obtain their independence, fought the Poles, who wanted to become masters of a region they'd once controlled. The Ukrainians were crushed. Then, when the Bolsheviks tried in their turn to conquer Galicia, the Poles repelled them. In two years, the Poles had played, successively, the roles of invader and protector against invaders even worse than themselves in the eyes of the Ukrainians.

Today, Polish-Ukrainian relations are good. The Polish domination of yesteryear is perceived by Lviv as a lesser evil. For lack of being able to agree on every detail, they at least are in agreement where their common enemy is concerned: the Russians. Rewriting the past has served to create a foundation for today's friendships and enmities. The "historic reconciliation" consists in restoring their revered status to those soldiers who died a century ago under contentious circumstances.

✦✦✦

The next day, I visit the Lviv History Museum to familiarize myself with the current reading being given to this troubled past. In the first room devoted to twentieth century history, I stumble upon a word in this explanatory note:

> On November 1st, 1918, the Central Military Committee headed by Dmytro Vitovsky, centurion of the Sich Riflemen, staged a military coup in Lviv that resulted in shifting control of the city

to Ukrainians, and hence a revolt of Polish <u>forces</u>, who claimed Galicia.

I notice that, curiously, "forces" has been added to the text with a strip of paper. Looking more closely, I see that I can make out, behind the paper, the original word that has been replaced: "chauvinists." That is the way, even recently, these same soldiers were described, who have just reassumed their glorious status in the Lychakiv Cemetery, and at the same time, in the history of Lviv.

If ever Polish-Ukrainian relations were to deteriorate, all they'd have to do would be to remove the strip of paper.

★★★

What will the history books say about you, Tyomochka, in ten, twenty, or a hundred years? Whose victim will you have been? And of what? Will your memory also be shunted back and forth from one version of history to the other, as alliances and conflicts come and go?

One day, the schoolbooks in a reunified Ukraine may say that you were killed by "the Russian aggressor and its terrorist collaborators" during "the Donbas occupation" before its "liberation" by the "patriotic Ukrainian forces." Or, if not, it will be the history books of the "Novorossiya Republic" that will present you as one of the victims of the genocidal policies of the fascist Ukrainian regime against Russian speakers" at the time of the "Donbas war of independence." In either case, the true circumstances of your death will have little influence on your place in history. You'll be buried in a common memorial grave in the name of the victor's version. The best scenario would be a stalemate, in which case you would be recognized as one of the too numerous victims of "the madness of men." They will say that there must "nevermore" be such a "national tragedy." No one will be judged for your death, but that will be the price to pay in order that only the losers be taken to task for their crimes. Believe me, my dear Artyom, it's really the best that the future has to offer you. Otherwise you'll be exposed to an endless exploitation of your memory; one day serving as fuel for the hatred of these against those, and the next day, of those against these.

Given all that, isn't it better to have died for nothing?

EPILOGUE

FOR WANT OF A FIR TREE

I now know that there is no happiness in hatred.

ALBERT CAMUS

I'm about to leave Ukraine. I've been here for a month. You've been dead for three weeks. I call your father for news. He's at the hospital, with your mother and your brother. The doctors have been able to save Misha's eye. "The shrapnel is lodged in his head, but he remembers everything. He never lost consciousness. I waited before telling him, but now he knows that his little brother is dead." Your mother is trying to get used to her phantom limb, says your father. "Imagine, thirty years with two legs, then they cut one off."

The foundry has offered him a room in one of their houses. But the street it's on has been recently bombed. He still prefers to sleep at the hospital. In recent days, the proud worker that he is has decided to accept the material aid offered by humanitarian organizations. "Before, I didn't want to receive anything from anyone. I got by on my own. I told myself that others were more in need than me. Now, I can't refuse anything. I've nothing left."

Your death has had repercussions in the media that have been painful for your father. "They wrote that after what happened, I wanted to join the rebels. It's not true. I couldn't be part of an army, because I'd be incapable of killing people." He also saw on the Internet the photo I took of you in your coffin, with the Grads in the background. He did not appreciate that. Journalistically speaking, I feel that it was appropriate. But in his place, I would not have liked it either. The rocket launchers profane your death, politicize it, water down your father's grief, placing it in a context that is wider and more complex. He has enough to manage with his grief.

This photograph has circulated widely since I posted it on social media. However, those who have shared it have often taken the liberty of altering the description I made so that it will match their own biases. I specified that you had "probably" been killed by Ukrainian fire. *Probably*, because I could confirm nothing with absolute certainty. The pro-rebels deleted my qualification. The pro-Ukrainians, for their part, declined to be specific concerning the circumstances of your death, so as to be able to attribute it automatically to the separatists. A photographer colleague has also published photos of your funeral, but without the Grads, and without the *probably*. Not to support the rebels, but because logic has left little room for error, even without tangible proof. The Ukrainian ministry of defence has complained to the press agency that circulated those images, and has threatened to make trouble for him.

At the morgue, while waiting for your body, your father had told me that there was no military target in your neighbourhood at the time of the attack. On the telephone, I tell him about the separatist positions I saw in the street adjacent to yours, when I went to inspect the ruins of your house, right after the funeral. "Next to our neighbourhood, there's a no man's land of 2.5 square kilometres. It's true, rebel artillery fired from there. But where else could they go to defend us? We're in a city. There are residential areas everywhere. The rebels have to respond, otherwise the Ukrainian army will raze Donetsk in no time. The Ukrainians could have fired on the separatist positions in the no man's land. Their attack would have been justifiable. But they deliberately bombed our houses, the bastards." Your father has made his choice: the Ukrainians are the murderers, the rebels, his protectors. One way, perhaps, to give meaning to your death.

Recently, a bureaucrat from the Russian health ministry contacted him. He'd heard the story of your family on television, and promised that your mother could soon be transferred to Russia to be treated at the state's expense. Your father is preparing to move there for good, with what remains of your family. He's convinced that he'll be able to get along, because he's a worker, and workers always find a way to survive. On the other hand, he categorically excludes the idea of seeking refuge in the non-rebel regions of Ukraine, even though he's a citizen of that state. "Do you want me to go and have myself killed in the country that decimated my family? I don't want to be Ukrainian any more."

For him, the rupture is final. Whether the separatist territories are one day reunited with Ukraine or not, that country will never again be his native land. Because you will never be *reunited with life.*

FOR WANT OF A FIR TREE

★★★

I fly out of Ukraine on a Sunday afternoon. A piece of paper is claiming that last night at midnight, the weapons were to have gone silent in Donbas.

In the night of Wednesday to Thursday, in a neighbouring country, four men and one woman spent hours behind closed doors drinking coffee and negotiating. The next day, they announced that they had arrived at an agreement. The fighting would go on for three more days, and then a cease fire would come into effect, and it would stop. The two enemy leaders even shook hands for the occasion, though it's true, without much conviction.

Last night at midnight, nothing happened. The war was not yet ready to die. Everyone knew it. But some wanted to be able to say that they at least tried to halt it. Others wanted to gain time, and to give the illusion that they meant well.

This was not the right time. But one day, inevitably, the fighting will come to an end, out of breath, out of munitions, or out of justifications.

On that day, the Artyoms of four years, four months, and fourteen days, will no longer have their lives stolen from them by misdirected rocket fire.

On that day, I'll think of you, and of all that ought never to have happened.

Starting with the beginning.

For want of a fir tree, the peace was lost.
For want of peace, the balance was lost.
For want of balance, unity was lost.
For want of unity, the peninsula was lost.
For want of the peninsula, the east was lost.
For want of the east, thousands of lives were lost.

All that for a simple fir tree.

POSTSCRIPT

Since my visit to Ukraine in January and February of 2015, the toll of victims in the Donbas conflict has more than doubled. From time to time, heightened tensions slightly shift the front line, sometimes in favour of the pro-Russian rebels, sometimes to the advantage of the Ukrainian forces. In Kyiv, the heroes of the Revolution of Dignity are at each others' throats. Corruption, authoritarianism, and the wielding of arbitrary power
are overwhelming hopes for a better future. Otherwise, nothing has really changed. The country is still divided. Crimea is still under Russian control. Hatred of the Other remains a proof of patriotism. The launchers of bombs are still convinced that their cause is just. And Artyom is still dead.

ACKNOWLEDGMENTS

To

Zee, for the past, present, and future;
Jas, for brotherhood, passion, thoughtfulness;
Mom and *Pop*, for life, care, love
Laeti, for solidarity, affection, sharing;
Sashenka, for exactness, promptness, friendship;
Bruno, for the years, honesty, words;
Tash, *Cath*, *Hum*, for the wine, shelter, courage;
Henrik, for the couch, the walks, the laughter;
Renard and Mylène, for the vision, the confidence, the lighthouse;
And *Don and Linda*, for the kindness, the translation, the second life.

Thank you.